J.O.S.E.P.H.

A pathway to wealth

A person's gift opens doors for him and
brings him before the great.

ETS Publishing

JOSEPH: A Pathway to Wealth
© 2025 by Elim Twelve Seventy Publishing

Scripture quotations are taken from the Holy Bible, New International Version®, NIV®. Copyright © 1973, 1978, 1984, 2011 by Biblica, Inc.™ Used by permission. All rights reserved worldwide.

ISBN: 979-8-9934876-0-1
Published by Elim Twelve Seventy Publishing
www.twelveseventy.com

Wealth is a

Journey of Owning your gift to provide Solutions, Expand kingdom influence, and create Perpetual income that Honors God

Contents

Chapter One

Journey of Mind Renewal

Introduction

Lasting wealth doesn't come from quick fixes or overnight miracles. It's a journey; one that involves process, pruning, and purposeful growth. Whether you're looking at Scripture or real-life examples today, true abundance is rarely instant. It comes through seasons of preparation, obedience, and transformation.

Take Abraham, he waited and wandered for years before stepping into God's promise. David was anointed long before he was appointed, going through betrayal, caves, and hidden seasons. Even today, those who've built lasting, generational wealth will tell you it came through years of learning, serving, failing forward, and staying aligned with purpose.

As a believer and as someone who understands both the numbers and the narratives, I've come to see that wealth in God's Kingdom is never just about accumulation. It's about trust. It's about stewardship. It's about purpose. Before Joseph ever stepped into influence in Egypt, before he interpreted dreams or managed resources at a national level, he was first shaped through God's process. His promotion was never just about personal success; it was about Kingdom impact.

Biblical wealth isn't about chasing money. It's about becoming the kind of person God can entrust with responsibility and resources. In this first chapter, we'll look at the spiritual purpose of wealth, God's heart behind provision, and the foundation for what I call the Joseph Blueprint, a faith-rooted, purpose-driven approach to prosperity.

Why Wealth Matters in the Kingdom

A well-known pastor in the Haitian community had a bold vision: to build a state-of-the-art church facility equipped with high-tech features and multiple rooms designed for events, education, and outreach. His heart was clear— *"I want to offer Jesus the best that the market can provide."* This wasn't about extravagance; it was about excellence for the Kingdom.

Determined to pursue the vision with diligence, he gathered a team and developed a comprehensive, professional business plan. The plan was meticulously reviewed by certified public accountants, architects, and marketing experts to ensure it met both ministry needs and financial standards. Confident in the strength of his proposal, he approached the bank for financing, believing it would be a straightforward approval.

To his surprise, the first bank denied his request. He remained undeterred. *"Even great projects face rejection,"* he reasoned. But then the second bank said no. Then the third. One by one, rejection after rejection came in. Seventeen banks later, he still hadn't received the funding. What began as a confident expectation turned into a season of testing and doubt.

Throughout my lifelong involvement in church, I've witnessed countless stories like this where people with powerful vision and genuine passion for the Kingdom of God were hindered, not by lack of commitment, but by a lack of financial resources. Many local churches remain stagnant due to a lack of resources to move forward. Others slowly fade away, unable to meet ongoing financial obligations.

I've seen men and women of God, humble, faithful, and deeply in love with God, driven by selfless desires to serve their communities. Yet, they're often met with a harsh reality: financial obstacles that seem insurmountable. How many families remain broken because they can't afford counseling or legal help? How many children miss out on their education because tuition is out of reach? How many Kingdom dreams never leave the paper because money stands in the way like a giant, immovable, intimidating, and unclaimed?

These aren't just financial issues; they are vision barriers. And until we learn to break the mindset of scarcity, fear, and passivity and embrace Kingdom stewardship, we will continue to watch extraordinary callings stall at the gates of lack.

During my college years, a professor once shared a thought that left a lasting impression on me. He said that when we assess the cost of war, we typically focus on tangible losses, the number of lives lost, the destruction of infrastructure, and the military expenses incurred. But one cost often goes uncounted: the cultural cost.

He challenged us to consider the unseen casualties, the children who never returned to school, the students whose education was permanently disrupted, or the potential that was buried beneath the rubble. What about the future doctors who never discovered a cure because their training was cut short? How many Picassos or Michelangelos, how many Einsteins or Messis were silenced before they ever picked up a brush, wrote a formula, or kicked a soccer ball simply because their lives were claimed or redirected by conflict? Then he concluded with a sobering truth: "The damage to lives and buildings may be measured during the war, but the loss of knowledge and culture is felt for generations." His words opened my eyes to a deeper reality: not all losses are visible, and not all costs can be counted in dollars or bodies. Some costs echo silently through history, robbing the world of what could have been.

Novak Djokovic is a powerful example of what the world could have lost to war. During his childhood in Serbia, his life was constantly under threat. He grew up in a middle of a war. And yet, despite those circumstances, he rose from the rubble to become one of the greatest athletes in history. Today, Novak Djokovic holds the record for the most Grand Slam titles won (24), 100 career titles, and the most Masters-1000 wins. His epic rivalries with Roger Federer and Raphael Nadal elevated the sport to new heights. For many, he is the greatest tennis player ever to live. Djokovic's legacy goes beyond trophies. He has sponsored hundreds of children, opened training centers, and created countless opportunities for the next generation. His impact is not just athletic; it is generational.

Now pause and consider: what if one bullet had struck him as a child? What if he had been captured, silenced, or locked down by fear and chaos? None of those accomplishments would exist. The world would have lost not just a champion but a legacy.

In ministry, we often count what's obvious: the buildings we can't finish, the outreaches we cancel, or the equipment we lack. But rarely do we stop to calculate the hidden cost of financial limitation.

How many anointed men and women of God never launched their ministry? How many Kingdom projects were buried because of a lack of funding? This is the silent war on purpose, where visions die in the planning stage, not because they weren't from God, but because the people of God hadn't yet learned to steward, fund, and invest in what matters most.

So it's time to break the silence. We can't afford to ignore this unseen battle any longer. We need both spiritual wisdom and practical strategy to face it head-on. Because if we don't confront the financial barriers in ministry, we'll keep losing ground we didn't even realize was ours to take. There's more God wants to entrust to us, but we have to be ready to steward it.

Why does Wealth Matter in the Kingdom? The answer is simple. Wealth matters because it empowers the advancement of God's work on earth. It enables us to make Christlike disciples, fulfill the mandate to take dominion (Genesis 1:26), and leave a lasting impact on generations to come.

With financial resources, we can build orphanages, plant and grow churches, equip leaders, train disciples, educate communities, and elevate the quality of life for those in need. Wealth fund vision. It turns ideas into action and purpose into progress. And the list doesn't end there; it continues as long as there are people to reach, souls to save, and lives to transform.

God's work is spiritual, but it moves through the material. Without resources, even the most incredible vision remains grounded. Wealth in the hands of the righteous fuels transformation that reaches far beyond one lifetime; it touches generations.

When someone has been conditioned by years of financial struggle, living paycheck to paycheck, stretching every dollar, or tirelessly raising funds for ministry, it becomes difficult to envision abundance as part of God's plan. The weight of survival often distorts expectation, making wealth feel foreign, even unspiritual.

Yet the Bible paints a very different picture. Scripture presents a clear pattern: God has always entrusted significant resources to those called to fulfill substantial assignments. The wealth described in the Bible is immense, strategic, and often generational.

We see this principle woven throughout Scripture. Abraham, for example, was "very rich in livestock, silver, and gold" (Genesis 13:2), but his wealth didn't define him; it served God's purposes. He built altars, honored the Lord, and became a blessing to others. Solomon, too, used his God-given wisdom and wealth to build the temple, establishing Israel's influence among the nations. In the New Testament, Joseph of Arimathea, another wealthy man, didn't just hold influence; he used it. He offered his own tomb for the body of Jesus, fulfilling prophecy at a pivotal moment in redemptive history. Riches didn't drive these men, but they empowered them. Their wealth wasn't about status but about stewardship. And truth be told, the scale of their resources would rival or even exceed many of today's wealthiest individuals.

Example: David and His Soldiers – 1 Chronicles 29. If we want a picture of what Kingdom wealth looks like in action, we don't have to look any further than King David and his leaders. In 1 Chronicles 29, we see one of the most powerful displays of what happens when spiritual vision meets financial stewardship. David knew the temple had to be built—but he also knew he wouldn't be the one to build it. Still, he didn't sit back. He stepped up. Scripture tells us in *1 Chronicles 29:4* that David gave *3,000 talents of gold (from Ophir) and 7,000 talents of refined silver* to cover the temple walls. When you convert that to today's values, you're talking about more than $6.81 billion USD—a staggering offering from one man.

But here's what's even more powerful: David's giving sparked a chain reaction. In *verses 6–9*, we see Israel's leadership rise. The tribal officers, military commanders, and family leaders followed David's example, giving out of what they already had. Together, they gave 5,000 talents and 10,000 darics of gold, 10,000 talents of silver, 18,000 talents of bronze, and 100,000 talents of iron. Just the gold alone would be worth over $11 billion today. The silver? More than $255 million. And that doesn't even include the bronze and iron, which, in that day, held immense strategic and military value.

This wasn't emotional giving. It was strategic. It was intentional. It was legacy-minded. These men didn't give because they were pressured. They gave because they had been prepared. Years of stewardship made this moment possible. Their giving didn't come from lack—it came from overflow. And the result was historic: they helped lay the financial and spiritual foundation for the temple of God.

There's a truth here we can't ignore: you can't give what you don't have, and you won't have what you don't steward. God's work often advances through the hands of people He has already blessed.

Moses and the Israelites – Exodus 25 & 35: Provision with a Purpose

One of the most powerful pictures of Kingdom provision shows up in an unexpected place, in the wilderness. When God gave Moses the blueprint for the tabernacle, His presence wasn't going to dwell in just any structure. It had to be holy, intentional, and built with purpose. But here's what's remarkable: God didn't rain down supplies from heaven. He gave the people an opportunity to participate.

In *Exodus 25:2*, God says, "Tell the Israelites to bring me an offering. You are to receive the offering for me from everyone whose heart prompts them to give." This wasn't about pressure. It was about posture. God wasn't demanding; they were invited. He asked for offerings from those whose hearts were stirred, who were moved not by guilt, but by vision.

But don't miss this: they already had what they needed. Back in Exodus 12:35-36, when the Israelites were leaving Egypt, God gave them favor with their oppressors. The Egyptians handed over gold, silver, and delicate fabric, plunder in the eyes of man, but provision in the eyes of God. What they thought was back pay for slavery was actually seed for the sanctuary. What looked like overflow from their past was preparation for their future.

Fast forward to *Exodus 35*, and you see a nation come alive with generosity. Men and women, young and old, began bringing gold earrings, rings, silver, bronze, fine linen, dyed yarn, animal skins, precious stones, and even acacia wood. Others stepped up with skills: spinning, sewing, crafting, and building. They gave not only from their physical resources, but from their gifts and abilities as well.

To put this in perspective with modern values: If just 1,000 people gave half an ounce of gold each (about 14 grams), at $65 per gram, that's over $900,000 USD, just from jewelry. Silver, bronze, precious materials, and craftsmanship would easily push the collective value into the millions.

1. Provision flows through people, not down from the sky.
    Yes, God is always the ultimate source. But more often, He releases His provision through *people*, not apart from them. When it was time to build the temple, gold didn't fall from heaven. Instead, God stirred the hearts of His people to give generously from what they already had. The same with the tabernacle, God invited Israel to partner with Him, not just in spirit, but in substance.

2. Wealth is meant for worship. In *1 Chronicles 29:14*, David prays, *"But who am I, and who are my people, that we should be able to give as*

generously as this? Everything comes from you, and we have given you only what comes from your hand." This wasn't a king boasting—it was a worshipper bowing. David understood something we must reclaim today: wealth isn't just for comfort, control, or legacy. Wealth is a tool for worship. When David gave, it wasn't just a donation; it was devotion. His offering was spiritual before it was financial. The same truth held in Moses' day. He knew that every resource in the people's hands: their gold, silver, cloth, even their creativity, was already a gift from God. So when they gave, they weren't giving something away; they were giving something back. They gave with reverence and with joy, because they knew the source and the purpose of what they carried.

Example: Billy Graham – Stewarding Wealth for Worship and Kingdom Impact

When we talk about modern evangelism, one name consistently rises to the forefront: Billy Graham. Over the course of his life, he preached the gospel to more than 215 million people in over 185 nations—from dusty village roads to global stadiums, from military fields to presidential offices. But what many don't see behind the crowds and conversions is the Kingdom infrastructure that made it all possible.

Billy Graham understood a foundational truth: the gospel is free, but getting it to the nations requires faithful stewardship. Preaching to the masses involved

11

funding airplanes, radio, and TV broadcasts; printing millions of tracts and Bibles; mobilizing teams; securing venues; and following up with new believers. This wasn't about chasing money—it was about channeling resources for Kingdom advancement.

Each crusade wasn't just an event; it was a full-scale mission. Stadiums were filled with people, but with prayer, planning, and provision. A single event could cost between $2 million and $6 million in today's value. Over 400 crusades, media outreach, and global discipleship efforts, the total Kingdom investment easily reaches into the multi-billion-dollar range. But every dollar had one assignment: advance the gospel and glorify God.

What made Graham's approach so powerful wasn't just his global reach—but his integrity. He stewarded finances as an act of worship. He kept his own salary modest. He refused personal offerings. He surrounded himself with accountability and transparency, not for appearance—but out of reverence for the call.

Billy Graham didn't view money as a trophy. He saw it as a tool, a sacred trust to carry the gospel to the ends of the earth. Every donation was treated as holy. Every partner was viewed as a co-laborer. And every campaign was planned with a heart of honor.

This is the model: worship through stewardship— Kingdom expansion through financial integrity. Graham's legacy isn't just etched in history books—it lives on in the lives changed, the churches planted, the leaders equipped, and the gospel still advancing today.

God Uses People to Fund His Kingdom

Throughout Scripture and history, one truth remains consistent: God advances His Kingdom through people, and that includes their money.

From David's temple to Moses' tabernacle, from the generosity of the Israelites to the global crusades of Billy Graham, we see the same pattern God provides. Still, He gives through willing hearts and faithful hands. He doesn't drop gold from the sky; He deposits it into the lives of stewards who understand their role in His plan.

This isn't just about giving, it's about kingdom responsibility. In Genesis 1:26, God gave humanity a divine mission: *"Let them have dominion..."* Dominion requires more than good intentions. It requires resources, influence, and capacity. Christians cannot fulfill their assignment to lead, build, restore, and disciple nations without the means to do so.

Wealth Is First a Mindset

Before wealth ever arrives in your hands, it must first take root in your mindset. True prosperity doesn't start with a bank deposit; it begins with a mental shift.

Proverbs 23:7 says, *"As a man thinketh in his heart, so is he."* This means your internal beliefs will shape your external reality. If deep down you believe that wealth is sinful, unreachable, or "not for people like me," then even if God opens a door, you may subconsciously sabotage it. You'll either avoid opportunities, mismanage provision, or reject financial responsibility out of guilt or fear.

This is why renewing your mind is the *first step* toward walking in God's provision. Romans 12:2 urges us to be transformed by the renewing of our minds so we can discern God's will, which includes His desire to bless and entrust resources to His children.

Over the years, I've encountered countless Christians who pray fervently, worship passionately, and faithfully attend church meetings. Many are diligent in reading the Bible daily. Yet, I've noticed that few truly commit to the practice of renewing their minds. Renewing the mind is more than acquiring biblical knowledge; it's about replacing old, worldly patterns of thinking with God's truth. It's not just an intellectual exercise; it's a spiritual transformation that reshapes our thoughts so they align with God's perspective and ultimately, lead to a transformed life.

Both of my parents passed away from illness within a year of each other, after 43 years of marriage. I still vividly remember the moment my father died in our living room. At that time, I was a committed Christian, and I wasn't attending church just because of tradition or family expectations. I had already made my faith personal. I remember sitting on the floor that day, heartbroken, thinking, *"If only I could do something."* Deep down, I believed that dying from disease was not

God's perfect will, but I didn't yet have a clear understanding of his ideal will: the mind of Christ. My mind hadn't been renewed enough to discern or act on God's will concerning healing confidently.

In 2014, after my eight siblings and I buried our mother, I made a personal vow: I would discover God's perfect will regarding healing. For the next six months, I devoted myself entirely to this pursuit, reading Scripture, listening to teachings, and studying everything I could on the subject. That season became a turning point in my life. What began as a search became a transformation. I no longer wrestle with doubt about God's heart for healing. I am now fully convinced by His Word. My life, especially in this area, has been transformed through the renewing of my mind.

In 2016, I was diagnosed with kidney stones in both kidneys. The pain was intense—relentless. But by that time, my mind had already been renewed to the truth about divine healing, the finished work of Christ, and the power of communion. I did not doubt in my heart that it was God's will for me to be healed. I knew He wanted me pain-free and my kidneys whole and fully functional. One day, fed up with the discomfort, I decided to act on what I believed. I was at work, so I grabbed a piece of bread and substituted orange juice for wine, simple elements, but with sacred meaning. I took communion by faith. Nothing happened in that moment, no feelings, no goosebumps, no visible sign. But I didn't need one. My mind was already aligned with God's Word. I knew His will.

Two weeks later, I went in for a medical checkup. The results? Both of my kidneys were completely healed, healthy, and whole. Not a trace of the stones remained.

Looking back, I realize the healing had always been God's will. The only thing blocking it was my old way of thinking. My unbelief, rooted in worldly ideas and limited theology, had become a barrier. But once that mindset was broken and truth took its place, healing flowed freely.

God never changed. He was ready to heal all along. It was my renewed mind that unlocked what was already mine in Christ.

Over the years, I've come to realize that very few Christians operate with a truly renewed mind when it comes to healing, and even fewer when it comes to money. While many are sincere in their faith, their thinking in these areas is often shaped more by tradition, fear, or personal experience than by Scripture. When it comes to money, I've seen believers embrace dangerous misconceptions like: wealth is inherently sinful, money is a trap leading to spiritual downfall, or poverty somehow equals piety. Some even believe that God's perfect will for their life includes struggle and financial lack as if scarcity were more spiritual than abundance.

But I know firsthand that these beliefs are not rooted in the heart of God; they are strongholds that must be broken. Just as I confronted and rejected the mindset that sickness was a normal or acceptable part of life for a believer, I had to renew my thinking about money through the truth of God's Word. I came to see that both healing and provision are part of the covenant promises of God, and that ignoring either one is to live beneath the fullness of what Christ paid for.

And just like healing, financial renewal doesn't happen by accident. It requires intentional study, prayer, and alignment with the principles of the Kingdom. Through my own journey, I've identified three major mental strongholds that continue to hinder God's people from walking in abundance. These deeply ingrained patterns of thought must be uprooted and replaced with truth if we are to fully step into the financial freedom and purpose God has designed for us.

Breaking the mindset of scarcity

Many sincere believers unknowingly operate with a poverty mindset; a way of thinking rooted in survival, scarcity, and fear. This mindset doesn't always sound negative. In fact, it often wears the disguise of humility. It says things like:

- "Just enough is good enough."

- "My treasure is in heaven; this earth is just a bridge."

- "Money will only make me proud or draw me away from God."

These phrases aren't usually spoken with rebellion; they come from genuine devotion and often from people who genuinely love God. I've heard them countless times, and often from individuals who are prayerful, faithful, and even sacrificial in their service. Yet beneath their sincerity is a silent agreement with lack, as though poverty itself is a form of righteousness.

What makes this mindset even more challenging is that it often hides behind Scripture. Verses like *Proverbs 30:9*, "...give me neither poverty nor riches...," or the parable of the rich man and Lazarus are commonly quoted to suggest that scarcity is somehow spiritual, or that lack is a pathway to inheriting the Kingdom. But taken out of context, these passages can lead believers to embrace limitation instead of pursuing Kingdom purpose.

These Scriptures were never meant to glorify poverty or cast suspicion on prosperity. They are warnings—not about the provision itself, but about misplaced trust. They confront the dangers of greed and self-reliance, not the blessing of godly abundance. The issue isn't wealth, it's the heart behind it. These texts speak to motives, not means, to purpose, not possessions. Let's take a closer look at the parable of the rich man and Lazarus and see what Jesus was really addressing.

The story of the rich man and Lazarus in Luke 16:19-31 is often quoted in isolation, but its real meaning becomes clearer when we look at the whole chapter. Jesus doesn't start with that story; He begins in verse 1 by addressing His disciples with a parable about a rich man's manager who was accused of wasting his master's possessions. From the very beginning, Jesus is teaching about mismanagement, accountability, and the proper use of resources. The dishonest manager, once exposed, takes quick action, not to save his job, but to build goodwill. And surprisingly, Jesus praises his shrewdness, not his dishonesty. He then says, *"Use worldly wealth to gain friends for yourselves, so that when it is gone, you will be welcomed into eternal dwellings."* (Luke 16:9). In other words, use money wisely, in a way that honors eternal values and blesses people.

Then in verses 13 to 15, Jesus delivers a direct warning: *"You cannot serve both God and money."* He was addressing people who were not just wealthy, but in love with wealth, namely, the Pharisees. Verse 14 makes this crystal clear: *"The Pharisees, who loved money, heard all this and were sneering at Jesus."*

It's essential to recognize the structure of Luke 16. Verses 1–15 deliver strong teachings on stewardship, integrity, and the danger of greed. Jesus addresses the misuse of wealth, the love of money, and the inability to serve both God and riches. Then, beginning in verse 19, Jesus transitions into a powerful parable that illustrates the eternal consequences of ignoring everything He just taught. It's as if He's saying: *"If you choose to live like those I just described, hoarding wealth, ignoring the needy, and allowing money to master your heart, this is the outcome you can expect."*

The rich man in the parable is the embodiment of that warning. Look closely at verses 19–21: *"There was a rich man who was dressed in purple and fine linen and lived in luxury every day. At his gate was laid a beggar*

19

named Lazarus, covered with sores and longing to eat what fell from the rich man's table. Even the dogs came and licked his sores." Day after day, this wealthy man saw Lazarus sick, hungry, suffering, yet he did absolutely nothing. His sin wasn't just in what he did, but in what he refused to do. His heart was so consumed with his own comfort and lifestyle that he became blind to the desperation at his own doorstep.

The parable of the rich man and Lazarus is not a condemnation of wealth; it's a warning against the *misuse* of it. Jesus wasn't teaching that riches are inherently evil or that poverty is intrinsically righteous. He was exposing the danger of a heart disconnected from compassion, a life misaligned with purpose, and a mindset closed off to the needs of others.

Many sincere believers have adopted a poverty mindset, not out of rebellion, but due to a misplaced humility that believes lack somehow honors God more than abundance. But Scripture doesn't celebrate lack; it calls for stewardship. It doesn't glorify scarcity; it champions generosity. The gospel is not advanced by what we refuse to have; it's advanced by what we are willing to release for God's glory.

The issue has never been about how much we have, but about *what we do with what we have.* The problem isn't prosperity, it's the absence of purpose. It's when wealth becomes our master instead of our servant. It's when we hoard instead of help, when we preserve instead of pour out.

God is not intimidated by wealth; He's the source of it. What He desires is people who are so aligned with His heart that every resource in their hands becomes an instrument of worship and a channel for Kingdom advancement.

So, let's break the agreement with the lie that poverty equals piety. Let's reject the fear that tells us prosperity will pull us from God. Instead, let's embrace the truth: we are blessed to be a blessing. Our provision has a purpose: *to reveal God's heart, to reach the lost, and to reflect His Kingdom on earth as it is in heaven.* And at the end, every believer should aspire to live a life that echoes the testimony of David: *"He died at a good old age, having enjoyed long life, wealth, and honor. His son Solomon succeeded him as king."* 1 Chronicles 29:28

Breaking the Mindset of Fear.

Many believers have unknowingly embraced a mindset rooted in fear; a fear that often disguises itself as reverence or humility, but in reality, holds them back from walking in the fullness of God's provision. This fear can take many forms: Fear of losing salvation, Fear of dishonoring God, Fear of being judged, punished, or disqualified for desiring financial success. Over time, these fears create a distorted belief system, one where lack is equated with holiness, and poverty is mistaken for piety.

Fear becomes one of the most significant spiritual roadblocks. It paralyzes faith, distorts theology, and limits potential. And as long as fear is in the driver's seat, many will remain stuck, believing that living small is somehow more pleasing to God. But God is not glorified by unused gifts, unfulfilled callings, or underdeveloped potential.

One of the clearest illustrations of this is found in the Parable of the Talents (Matthew 25:14-30). Jesus told this story to reveal how the Kingdom of God operates, especially when it comes to stewardship.

Overview of the Parable

A wealthy master goes on a journey and entrusts his possessions to three servants: one receives five talents, one receives two talents, and one receives one talent. It's important to note that a talent was a unit of money— approximately 20 years' worth of wages. In today's terms, even one talent would be the equivalent of hundreds of thousands of dollars. Each servant was given an amount "according to his ability." The master wasn't unfair; he entrusted them with what he believed they could manage.

It is interesting to see the wording used to explain the action of each servant. For the first ones, we read "they put their money to work and gained..." 5 more and two more for the second one. But the servant with one talent *buried it in the ground.*

When the master returned, he praised the first two as *"good and faithful servants."* He rewarded them with greater responsibility and invited them into *"the joy of the Lord."* But the third servant? He didn't lose money.

He didn't steal. He did nothing and yet, his master called him: *"Wicked and lazy servant."* (v. 26)

At the heart of every lesson in the Parable of the Talents is one central truth: your mindset determines your stewardship. This master, who is an image of God himself, is teaching the following:

- Fear Is Not an Excuse. The servant admitted: *"I was afraid and went and hid your talent in the ground"* (v. 25). This admission reveals a fear of failure. Fear of success. Fear of responsibility. All of these can lead us to bury what God intended to be sown.

- God Expects Multiplication, Not Just Maintenance. The servant wasn't punished for being reckless; he was punished for being unproductive. His mindset? He said, "Here is what belongs to you." Doing *nothing* with what God gives you is a form of disobedience.

- God Gives According to Capacity. Each person received a different amount, but all were judged by what they *did* with what they had. God isn't comparing your five to someone else's ten; He's asking if you're being faithful with your one. It's not about how much you have, but what you do with it.

- Unused Potential Gets Reassigned. The master took the one talent from the lazy servant and gave it to the one who had 10 (v. 28). This reveals a Kingdom principle: *"To the one who has, more will be given. But from the one who does not have, even what he has will be taken away.* (v. 29) God reallocates resources to those who will steward and multiply them; to those who take risks. If you won't invest your gift, your opportunity, or your money, it may be handed to someone who will. Many people lament that the rich keep getting richer while the poor stay poor, but perhaps the answer lies in this Kingdom principle.

Fear is not spiritual. It's a human emotion, a natural response meant to help us assess risk, not surrender to it. In the proper context, fear can alert us to danger. But when left unchecked, it becomes a mindset—one that limits vision, blocks obedience, and distorts our understanding of God's will.

Many believers have unknowingly allowed fear to shape their theology and stewardship. It sounds like reverence, but it's really resistance. It hides behind statements like, "I don't want to get ahead of God," or "What if I mess it up?" But the Parable of the Talents shows us that fear, when left to lead, produces disobedience. But the Kingdom doesn't move through fear; it moves through *faith*. God doesn't reward timidity; He honors trust. He calls us to act, to build, to invest, to grow what we've been given.

The truth is: God is not looking for perfection, He's looking for participation. You may not feel like you have much. But if you're faithful with your "one talent," He can multiply it beyond what you imagined. Unused potential doesn't glorify God; it delays His purpose. And when we consistently bury what God has placed in us, He may choose to put it in the hands of someone who will steward it boldly, not out of punishment, but out of principle.

The Kingdom advances through people who believe that what they carry matters. And fear, no matter how spiritual it may sound, will always be the enemy of faith, progress, and purpose. So today, break the agreement with the lie that playing small honors God. He is not glorified by buried gifts or quiet disobedience. He is glorified when His sons and daughters step out, trusting Him, using what they've been given, and multiplying it for eternal impact. *Now is the time to come out of hiding and put your talent to work.*

Breaking the mindset of passivity

Many Christians assume that financial blessings will overflow automatically simply by attending church, believing in God, and faithfully tithing. This mindset often takes on several forms, such as the belief that *"If I serve God with all my heart, He will make me wealthy." "If I consistently give tithes and offerings, my seed will grow until I become rich." "I've been faithful to God for years, surely, at some point, He owes me a financial breakthrough."*

These statements reflect sincere faith, and they are rooted in a genuine desire to honor God. However, they often overlook a vital truth: financial breakthrough is not just a result of devotion, it's a result of proper actions and diligence.

Tithing, giving, and spiritual obedience are essential, but they were never meant to replace practical principles like discipline, planning, budgeting, saving, and investing. Scripture shows us that God blesses faithfulness, but He also honors wisdom. Without applying these principles, even the sincerest believers can find themselves spiritually rich but financially stuck.

The story of the widow in 2 Kings 4 offers a sobering reminder: honoring God does not automatically shield us from financial hardship, especially when wisdom and planning are absent. In her desperation, the widow cried out to the prophet Elisha: *"Your servant, my husband, is dead, and you know that he revered the Lord. But now his creditor is coming to take my two boys as his slaves."* (v. 1). Her words reveal a profound tension. Her late husband was a devout, faithful man of God, known for revering the Lord. Yet despite his spiritual integrity, he died with unresolved debts. His love for God was genuine, but his financial preparation was inadequate.

While he had gone to be with the Lord, freed from the burdens of this world, his wife and children were left vulnerable. The very family he had likely prayed for and protected in life now faced the terrifying possibility of slavery, not because of evil, but because of a lack of stewardship.

This passage delivers a clear message: spiritual devotion must be partnered with practical responsibility. Loving God and being called by God do not excuse us from managing resources wisely. In fact, the greater the calling, the greater the need for careful stewardship.

If we do not learn to manage and multiply what God places in our hands, we risk leaving behind burdens instead of blessings. Good intentions are not a substitute for good stewardship. God's desire is not only that we walk in righteousness, but that we also walk in wisdom so that our legacy will reflect both our faith and our foresight.

Proverbs 13:22 says, *"A good person leaves an inheritance for their children's children."* Notice—it doesn't just say "children," but "children's children." That means what you build, what you steward, and what you leave behind should be strong enough to bless not just the next generation, but the one after that. This reflects God's heart for us to think generationally, to live and lead with legacy in mind. The story in 2 Kings reminds us that spiritual devotion doesn't cancel the need for financial wisdom. Legacy requires both. God doesn't just want us to pass down faith; He wants us to pass down *fruitfulness.*

On the contrary, let's take a look at Jacob. He had worked many years for Laban, who consistently tried to manipulate his wages. When Jacob finally negotiated to keep only the streaked, speckled, and spotted animals, he developed a plan. He took fresh branches from poplar, almond, and plane trees, peeled the bark to expose white stripes, and placed them in the watering troughs. This visual strategy influenced breeding, and over time, the strongest animals became part of Jacob's herd.

Here are the Key Lessons

1. Jacob Didn't Just Pray; He Planned. Jacob could have said, "God will provide," and done nothing, but instead, he used wisdom, observation, and effort. He understood breeding patterns and applied a method, even when he didn't control all outcomes. He trusted God but did his part.

2. Diligence is a Form of Faith. Jacob's actions show that faith is not idle. True belief in God's promises moves us to work strategically. His diligence was an act of stewardship, not striving; it was using what he had while trusting God with the results.

3. God blessed His Effort, not His passivity. Verse 43 says: *"In this way the man grew exceedingly prosperous and came to own large flocks..."* This confirms that God's blessing flowed through Jacob's obedience and action, not through passivity.

These passages dismantle the mindset that faith equals inactivity or passivity. It shows us that waiting on God doesn't mean doing nothing; it means working in alignment with God's promise, breaking the mentality of passivity.

God has a mindset of abundance.

God is a multiplier by nature, not by exception. From the very beginning of Scripture, His intent for humanity was not survival but expansion. *"Be fruitful and multiply"* (Genesis 1:28) was more than a command; it was a revelation of His character. He delights in increase, in taking what is placed in His hands and producing something far greater. Whether it was a garden that grew into nations, five loaves that fed thousands, or a remnant church that became a global movement, God has always multiplied what is yielded to Him.

He is not limited by economy, background, or scarcity. He is the Source, the Sustainer, and the Supplier. But His multiplication often flows through alignment. When our mindset begins to mirror His, when we think like stewards, plan like builders, and give like heirs, something begins to shift. Our resources take on eternal purpose. Our small becomes a seed. Our vision expands. God does not just bless unquestioningly; He multiplies through those who are mentally, spiritually, and strategically aligned with His Kingdom.

Unfortunately, many believers have been exposed to unbalanced teachings about money; either glorifying poverty as holy or glorifying wealth as proof of spirituality. Neither is true. The Bible teaches stewardship, generosity, and righteousness, not greed or guilt. Misunderstanding God's mindset will lead to a misunderstanding of money and wealth. We must return to a biblical understanding that wealth is a tool, not a god, and not a curse. Wealth is not proof of salvation, nor is poverty a mark of piety. However, with a proper understanding of wealth's purpose and a proper heart, wealth, salvation, love, righteousness, and honor can all coexist.

The story of Job boldly challenges the false idea that great wealth and deep reverence for God cannot exist in the same life. Job was a man of unshakable integrity, described as "blameless and upright," one who feared God and turned away from evil (Job 1:1). Yet, this same man was also the wealthiest in the East (Job 1:3). His estate included 7,000 sheep, 3,000 camels, 500 yoke of oxen, and 500 female donkeys; an empire that in today's market would exceed $33 million USD. Job wasn't corrupt. He wasn't greedy. He was holy and wealthy. He was a living proof that millions and morality can walk hand in hand, that prosperity doesn't have to poison purity. His wealth wasn't the root of his righteousness, but his righteousness was the foundation of his wealth.

Even after losing everything, Job's end was greater than his beginning. God restored him, doubling his possessions to include 14,000 sheep, 6,000 camels, 1,000 yoke of oxen, and 1,000 female donkeys—a portfolio worth more than $67 million USD today. This wasn't just a symbolic gesture. It was a tangible statement from heaven: you can fear God and still flourish. Job's suffering didn't cancel his destiny; it clarified it. His story reveals that divine favor doesn't always mean avoiding trials, but it does mean rising from them with more than you lost. Job teaches us that it's possible to live with millions in your hands and humility in your heart, to build wealth not through manipulation, but through character, obedience, and unwavering trust in God. Wealth with integrity isn't just possible, it's biblical.

Another powerful example of Kingdom provision is found in Acts 4:34-35: *"There was not a needy person among them. For as many as were owners of lands or houses sold them and brought the proceeds of what was sold and laid it at the apostles' feet, and it was distributed to each as any had need."* This was not a small offering; it was the result of believers who were already financially blessed. These were men and women who owned multiple properties, land, and assets, an uncommon reality in ancient times, where the majority of people lived day-to-day. To own even one house or field placed you above the economic average; to have excess property to sell meant these believers were functioning in a level of abundance and financial overflow.

In today's terms, selling a piece of land or a home could easily represent contributions in the hundreds of thousands or even millions of dollars. These believers were giving from surplus. And that surplus, when unified under the leadership of the apostles, produced a supernatural result: "there was not a needy person among them." A financially empowered community strategically eliminated poverty. A community rooted in wealth, integrity, reverence for God, and the power to work miracles, proving that all these virtues can coexist in harmony. They proved that millions in the hands of the righteous can become a ministry, that abundance mixed with obedience can erase lack, and that true prosperity is measured not just by what you keep, but by how many lives are lifted through what you give.

Of course, God knows that with finances, ministries can expand, communities can be restored, education can be advanced, and the gospel can be preached more effectively. Ecclesiastes 10:19 says, "Money answers all things." While that's not an excuse for greed, it's a recognition that impact costs something. The early church grew not just through miracles, but through generous giving. If we want to expand the Kingdom, we must put on the mind of Christ, the mind of God.

Here are several powerful examples of material and financial multiplication in the Bible, demonstrating how God blesses and multiplies resources when there is faith, obedience, and stewardship:

- The Widow of Zarephath – *1 Kings 17:8–16*. When Elijah asked a starving widow to give him bread during a famine, she only had a handful of flour and a little oil. But because she obeyed, her supply never ran out throughout the drought.

- Elisha and the Widow's Oil – 2 Kings 4:1–7. A widow facing debt and the loss of her sons cried out to Elisha. He told her to gather jars and pour her remaining oil. As she obeyed, the oil multiplied until every jar was full. She sold the oil, paid her debt, and lived off the rest.

- The Feeding of the 5,000 – *Matthew 14:13 21*. Jesus took five loaves and two fish, gave thanks, and broke them. Over 5,000 men (plus women and children) were fed, and 12 baskets of leftovers remained.

- The Feeding of the 4,000 – *Matthew 15:32–39*. Again, Jesus multiplies food to feed thousands. This time, seven baskets of leftovers were collected.

- Isaac's Harvest in Famine – *Genesis 26:1–13*. During a famine, Isaac sowed in the land and received a hundredfold return that same year. He became very wealthy in livestock, crops, and servants.

- Joseph in Egypt – *Genesis 41*. Joseph's wisdom during Egypt's years of abundance led to massive food reserves. This grain was later sold and traded, generating national wealth and saving nations from famine.

- Peter's Miraculous Catch of Fish – *Luke 5:1–11*. After toiling all night with no results, Peter obeys Jesus and casts his net again. He catches so many fish that the boats begin to sink.

- The Early Church's Resource Sharing – *Acts 4:32-37*. The early believers shared their possessions. Land and houses were sold, and the proceeds were distributed so no one lacked anything.

Wealth is a heart position.

In truth, the Bible is filled with people who walked intimately with God and were entrusted with extraordinary wealth. As mentioned earlier, figures like Abraham, David, and Solomon rank among the wealthiest individuals in human history, yet few would dare to claim a deeper relationship with God than they had. Their secret wasn't found in their possessions, but in their perspective.

They didn't worship wealth; they worshiped with their wealth. They saw resources as tools, not trophies. Their hearts were aligned with God's purpose, and as a result, He entrusted them with abundance. The key was that money didn't have them. Their mindset made the difference.

Let's take a closer look at some people's famous verses against wealth. *"Again I tell you, it is easier for a camel to go through the eye of a needle than for someone rich to enter the Kingdom of God."* Matthew 19:24

To understand this, we must examine the context of the story. It begins with a young man of great wealth approaching Jesus and asking, *"Teacher, what good thing must I do to get eternal life?"* (v. 16) This question reveals something subtle but significant: his mindset. He didn't ask how to know God more deeply, how to walk in obedience, or how to serve the Kingdom. His concern wasn't intimacy with the Father; it was securing *eternity* for himself. In essence, his question was, *"How can I live forever?"*, not *"How can I live for God?"*

Throughout Scripture, none of the great men of God began their relationship with such a question. They pursued purpose, not preservation. They sought a relationship, not a reward. But this young man, though sincere, was focused on performance and self-preservation as if eternal life were a transaction he could earn, just like his wealth.

Jesus, seeing straight into his heart, replied: *"If you want to be perfect, go, sell your possessions and give to the poor, and you will have treasure in heaven. Then come, follow me."* (v. 21) That was the moment of truth. Jesus touched the very thing the man treasured most—his wealth. Just as He had taught earlier in Matthew 6:21, *"For where your treasure is, there your heart will be also."* And right there, his heart was exposed. His genuine desire wasn't to follow God; it was to hold on to his riches *and* inherit eternal life. He wanted salvation without surrender, destiny without discipleship. *"When the young man heard this, he went away sad, because he had great wealth."* (v. 22) The young man left grieving not because Jesus rejected him, but because he was unwilling to let go. Scripture says,

It's no surprise, then, that Jesus turned to His disciples and said: *"Truly I tell you, it is hard for someone rich to enter the kingdom of heaven... It is easier for a camel to go through the eye of a needle."* But the key is not the wealth itself; it's the attachment to it. This isn't a condemnation of riches. It's a warning about idolatry, misplaced trust, and the kind of mindset that sees money as the master instead of the servant.

Your heart is the problem, not wealth. Throughout Scripture, we find powerful examples of men who chose God's mission over personal wealth or comfort, proving that true greatness is found in surrender, not status. Proving that the heart posture is what matters. Moses turned his back on the riches of Egypt, choosing instead to suffer with God's people because he valued purpose over luxury (Hebrews 11:25–26). The Apostle Paul, once a man of influence and religious prestige, counted all his earthly gains as loss for the sake of knowing Christ (Philippians 3:7). Elisha walked away from a prosperous farming business, burning his plow and sacrificing his oxen to follow the call of God (1 Kings 19:21). Similarly, the disciples—including Peter, James, and John—left behind their fishing enterprises. Matthew abandoned his lucrative tax office, all to follow Jesus with no guarantee of material reward (Luke 5:11, 28). Nehemiah, though entitled to wealth as a governor, refused to exploit his position, choosing reverence and justice over entitlement (Nehemiah 5:14-15). And above all, Christ Himself—though rich in glory—became poor for our sake, embracing the cross instead of a crown so that we might inherit true riches (2 Corinthians 8:9). Where is my heart? This is the real question you need to answer.

Aligning with Purpose Before Profit

Before we ever ask, "How can I get rich?" we must ask, "What am I called to steward?" This is exactly what

Joseph modeled. His journey didn't begin with ambition for power or wealth; it began with a dream that revealed a calling. Every season he faced, whether in the pit, Potiphar's house, or prison, was about stewarding his gift with excellence, even when it didn't look like success. When your heart is aligned with stewardship, wealth becomes a byproduct, not the pursuit.

If you're unsure where to begin, ask yourself: What has God placed in my hands right now? What are the opportunities, people, or responsibilities within my current season that I can manage more intentionally? Sometimes, your stewardship assignment starts with something as small as a job, a family role, a volunteer position, or even a recurring burden to help in a particular area. Faithfulness in small places often unlocks favor for larger assignments.

Below is a collection of prominent wealthy figures from Scripture whose lives reveal that true prosperity is not rooted in possessions, but in purpose. Each example includes their wealth, spiritual focus, and most importantly, the divine purpose for which God entrusted them with resources.

Name	Wealth Type	Spiritual Focus	God-Given Purpose
Abraham	Livestock, silver, gold, servants	Believed in God; trusted in the promise more than possessions	To become the father of many nations and walk by faith

Joseph	Managed Egypt's economy and grain reserves	Gave credit to God for wisdom; remained humble in power	To preserve nations during famine
Job	Thousands of livestock and great wealth	Blessed God in both loss and gain; never idolized his riches	To reveal faith under testing and God's power to restore
David	National treasures, temple resources	Acknowledged that all wealth came from God	To prepare for the building of God's temple
Solomon	Surpassed kings in gold, trade, influence	Asked for wisdom to lead, not wealth	To govern Israel with divine wisdom
Barnabas	Owned and sold land	Used wealth for the good of others; laid it at the apostles' feet	To strengthen and support the early church
Wise Men	Brought gold, frankincense, and myrrh	Bowed down and worshiped Jesus	To honor the newborn King and fund His early needs

Uncovering your God-given purpose is the key that unlocks a renewed and empowered mindset. Without purpose, wealth becomes either a burden or an idol, but when purpose is clear, money becomes a tool for mission. Purpose brings clarity, order, and direction. It turns financial resources into Kingdom solutions and transforms gain into giving. The individuals highlighted above were not just wealthy; they were purposeful. And it was that purpose that allowed them to view their wealth not as the prize, but as a provision for something greater. When you understand the purpose behind your provision, you begin to steward with wisdom, live with intention, and leave a lasting impact. At the same time, when your purpose becomes clear, the resources needed to fulfill it begin to flow. Purpose attracts provision, and provision, when rightly understood, fuels purpose. It works both ways.

Reflection and application Questions:

1. Have you identified your God-given purpose? If not, what steps are you taking to seek clarity?

2. Which biblical example in this chapter resonates most with your current journey—and why?

3. What would it look like for you to live intentionally, with both your purpose and your finances aligned under God's direction?

4. What limiting beliefs about wealth or success have you inherited or adopted that need to be challenged through Scripture?

5. How does your current mindset align with God's perspective on stewardship and abundance?

8. How can you shift your mindset to see provision as fuel for Kingdom purpose, rather than personal accumulation?

9. How would your daily actions change if you believed that wealth is a byproduct of obedience and purpose?

10. What habits or thought patterns need to shift for your mindset to reflect Kingdom principles about money and mission?

Take a moment to pray, journal, or discuss these questions with a mentor or group. Transformation begins when reflection leads to action.

Chapter Two

Owning Your Gift – From Discovery to Mastery

Introduction

Many Christians are unaware that they carry a gift within them. Others know they're gifted, yet still live in lack. That's because having a gift alone doesn't create wealth; systems, stewardship, and strategy do. The story of Joseph, the Hebrew dreamer, reveals timeless principles for turning a God-given gift into wealth and influence.

This chapter unpacks the full journey from recognizing your divine edge to developing it with excellence and ultimately to building a reputation of trust, service, and mastery that opens doors and sustains success.

Discover your Divine Edge

Joseph's story doesn't begin in the palace; it begins in the realm of vision. As a young man, Joseph began to dream. But these were no ordinary dreams; they carried prophetic weight and symbolic depth. While others slept and forgot, Joseph *saw* and *pondered*. He perceived layers of meaning that others overlooked. This was his divine edge, a God-given ability to see beyond the surface and interpret what was hidden to the natural eye.

This gift marked him; it was a grace he carried. Planted deep within him by God, this inner vision would one day unlock famine strategies, guide nations, and preserve the future of God's people. When Pharaoh's court was gripped by confusion and fear, it was Joseph's gift that brought clarity. He interpreted dreams no one else could understand and offered economic solutions no one else could conceive. His wisdom turned a coming crisis into a divine opportunity. Under Joseph's leadership, Egypt became the most prepared and prosperous nation in the region.

The impact didn't stop at Egypt's borders. Thanks to his gift for dream interpretation, which led him to a position, his family, including his father Jacob, his brothers, and their entire household, survived the famine. What looked like betrayal years earlier had actually been God's setup for preservation. As Joseph himself would later declare: *"God sent me ahead of you to preserve for you a remnant on earth and to save your lives by a great deliverance." (Genesis 45:7)*

That remnant was more than just a family; it was the nation of Israel in seed form. Without Joseph's ability, they would have starved. Without Joseph's gift, the twelve tribes would have scattered. And without Joseph's administrative skills, the lineage of Judah, the line from which Jesus would come, could have perished.

Think about it: Joseph's gift didn't just save him from prison or save a generation; it preserved a bloodline. That's how powerful a gift is. What we usually see as a cute little ability can position you in history to fulfill a role far greater than yourself.

But here's the truth: what Joseph carried is not exclusive to him. You have your very own divine edge, a unique grace placed within you by God. It may not manifest through dreams or visions, but it is just as powerful, just as purposeful. Maybe it's the way you teach with clarity, communicate with impact, organize with ease, or solve problems with insight. Perhaps it's how you inspire others, bring order to chaos, or create beauty out of brokenness. Your sense of fashion, your eye for design, your passion for dance or innovation, these aren't coincidences. They're clues to your calling.

God often hides treasure in earthen vessels (2 Corinthians 4:7). Gifts don't always look spiritual on the surface, but they are *deeply sacred* in function. God

43

rarely announces gifts with fireworks; instead, He embeds them within your wiring, your personality, your instincts, waiting to be discovered, refined, and activated.

The challenge for many believers is that they have been conditioned to think divine gifts must look like prophecy, tongues, healing, or working miracles; gifts we can exercise primarily within the four walls of the church. But that's only one part of the picture.

The Bible isn't just filled with prophets and miracle workers—it's full of people whose gifts were practical, artistic, strategic, and administrative. Take Bezalel, for example. When God commanded Israel to build the tabernacle—His holy dwelling place in the wilderness—Moses was overwhelmed. The blueprint was detailed, the materials were precious, and the work demanded nothing less than excellence. Imagine Moses looking around and thinking, *"Lord, how am I supposed to pull this off? These people were enslaved just weeks ago! Who among them has the skill, the vision, and the hands for something this sacred?"*

But God had already prepared a man for the mission. *"See, I have chosen Bezalel son of Uri, the son of Hur, of the tribe of Judah, and I have filled him with the Spirit of God, with wisdom, with understanding, with knowledge and with all kinds of skills to make artistic designs for work in gold, silver and bronze, to cut and set stones, to work in wood, and to engage in all kinds of crafts."(Exodus 31:2–5)*

Bezalel didn't hold a title. He didn't lead a tribe. He didn't preach sermons or part seas. But he was filled with the Spirit of God, and his *divine edge* was craftsmanship. He carried wisdom for design, precision in execution, and a spirit of excellence that turned raw materials into sacred beauty. His assignment was not behind a pulpit but behind a workbench. His gift didn't flow through words; it flowed through hands that shaped gold, set stones, carved wood, and brought God's vision into tangible form.

This is the beauty of divine gifting: what may look ordinary in human eyes becomes extraordinary when touched by the Spirit of God.

You may never lay hands on the sick, but your hands may build something that heals a generation. Your calling may not echo through a microphone, but it might reverberate through a system, a strategy, a business, or a blueprint. Whatever gift you have, it can still bring glory to God.

Glory! Let's talk a bit about this word. How does something bring glory to someone? How does an invention bring glory to the inventor?

An invention is more than a product; it reflects its inventor's genius, purpose, and creativity. Every time an invention fulfills its purpose, it testifies to the one who created it. The success of the invention always points back to the mind behind it. Think about it, every time a room lights up, whether in a hut or a skyscraper, it reminds the world of the man who dared to harness light.

The light bulb brings glory to Thomas Edison. The iPhone reflects the vision of Steve Jobs. Its sleek design, powerful interface, and global impact continually highlight his innovative mind even after his death. Millions never met him, but they honor his genius every time they use the device. Same thing for the airplane. It gives glory to the Wright brothers. Their risky experimentation changed the way humans move across the globe. Every flight today is a silent salute to their courage and vision. Every time an invention fulfills its purpose, it reflects the brilliance of its inventor and brings glory to the one who designed it.

Now, let's take this principle to the spiritual level: You are God's invention. *"For we are His workmanship, created in Christ Jesus for good works..."* *(Ephesians 2:10)*. The word *"workmanship"* in the original Greek is *poiēma*, the root of our English word poem. It speaks of something carefully crafted, skillfully formed, and intentionally designed. You are God's masterpiece. His original design. A living expression of His creativity and purpose. You are a custom creation, a divine idea wrapped in flesh, born for a specific mission on the earth.

In John 15:8, Jesus said: *"This is to my Father's glory, that you bear much fruit..."* In other words, when you live out your purpose, you glorify the One who created you. When you walk in what you were designed to do, when your life produces the results heaven intended, God gets the glory. Just like an invention brings honor to its inventor, your fruitfulness reflects the genius and goodness of your Creator. Every time you function in your gift, solve a problem, serve someone well, or bring transformation, you become a living testimony of God's wisdom and grace.

So how do you bring glory to your Inventor? When you teach with power and clarity, it points to the Teacher who wired your mind to be a teacher; when you organize chaos into systems, it reflects the divine order of the God who made the universe. When you build, write, serve, lead, heal, or solve problems, your fruit from your gift testifies to your Source. Bezalel brought glory to God not through preaching or prophecy, but by exercising his craftsmanship with excellence, precision, and purpose. His creativity became his worship, and his skill gave form to the sacred.

I've heard many Christians say, *"We were born to worship,"* or *"Our purpose is to glorify God."* And they're right. But too often, we've reduced worship and glorifying God to singing songs in church or lifting our hands in a service. While those expressions matter, they represent only a small part of what true worship entails. Biblically speaking, we glorify God not just with our voices, but with our lives. You glorify God when you walk in purpose. You glorify Him when you steward your gift with excellence. You glorify Him when your unique abilities are used to serve, solve, build, teach, or lead in ways that reflect His wisdom and creativity. The greatest worship you can offer is to become everything God created you to be.

Bezalel was not a unique case. Scripture reveals that God consistently anoints practical, creative, and leadership gifts to advance His Kingdom purposes. Each of the following individuals used their unique edge to fulfill their calling and, by doing so, to glorify God in the process:

- Daniel – Government and Strategy: His gift was wisdom; spiritual insight combined with administrative excellence. Daniel had the rare ability to discern dreams, interpret mysteries, and provide sound counsel under pressure. He was a governmental strategist, placed by God at the heart of empires. He understood laws, managed transitions, interpreted national crises, and influenced policies. His gift opened doors to kings' courts.

- Lydia – Commerce and Hospitality: Lydia was a successful businesswoman, a dealer in purple cloth, and her entrepreneurial gift opened doors for the early church. She used her resources and home to host Paul and other believers, making her house a strategic hub for ministry in Philippi. Her commerce and hospitality weren't separate from her calling; they were her calling. Through her generosity and service, God's work was advanced, and His people strengthened.

- Aquila and Priscilla – Skilled Trade and Teaching: As tentmakers, Aquila and Priscilla had both a trade and a ministry. Their business sustained them, and through it, they connected with Paul, supporting him both financially and relationally. But beyond their hands, they used their minds and hearts to disciple. They took

Apollos, an eloquent but theologically incomplete preacher, and taught him the way of God more accurately (Acts 18:26). Their dual gifting in trade and teaching shows how God uses skilled workers to shape the future of faith.

- Nehemiah – Leadership and Project Management: Nehemiah wasn't a prophet like Elisha or a warrior like David; he was an administrator, a planner, a man with vision and execution power. When Jerusalem lay in ruins, God used his leadership gift to rebuild not just walls but hope and identity. He organized teams, cast vision, coordinated resources, and led with prayerful urgency. His leadership glorified God by restoring what was broken and reviving a people who had lost their sense of purpose.

- Boaz – Business and Justice: Boaz was a landowner and businessman, but his most incredible legacy came through how he used his position and influence. With integrity and wisdom, he redeemed Ruth, protected her dignity, and preserved a family line that would eventually lead to King David and ultimately to Jesus Himself. Boaz's business dealings weren't just transactions; they were opportunities to demonstrate righteousness, compassion, and covenant faithfulness. Through his obedience, God's redemptive plan advanced.

Each of these individuals glorified God through their service, leadership, building, giving, and creation within their domain of influence. Your gift, no matter how "ordinary" you think it may seem, can do the same. Your skill is a tool; your work is worship, and your life, expressed through your gift, is a stage for God's glory.

Personal Reflection: My Journey of Gift Discovery As long as I can remember, math has always been my strength, but my real passion is teaching. When I discovered that it is my passion and gift, I went all in. In the beginning, it was in the classroom. I felt alive when I saw others grasp new concepts—when understanding sparked in their eyes. I realized my calling wasn't just about transferring knowledge but about transforming lives. That passion has since taken me far beyond the classroom—but it all began there.

5 Steps to Help You Discover Your Gift

Every person carries a unique potential—something that sets them apart and adds value to the world. Discovering your gift isn't about chasing trends or comparing yourself to others; it's about paying attention to the clues already present in your life. Here are five thoughtful steps to help uncover what's been inside you all along.

1. Pause and Reflect Deeply

In the noise of everyday life, it's easy to overlook what's within us. Creating space for quiet reflection can reveal the things that truly matter to you.

- Ask yourself: *What activities bring me energy, joy, or peace?*

- Consider what you've always loved doing—even if no one else noticed.

- Pay attention to what you naturally think about, dream of, or are drawn to.

2. Explore Your Story and Strengths

Your past carries clues to your design. Often, your gift has already shown up in your life—you didn't recognize it at the time.

- Look for moments where you felt confident, practical, or valuable.

- What challenges have you overcome, and what did they reveal about you?

- Identify recurring themes—ways you've helped, led, supported, or created.

3. Listen to Honest Feedback

Sometimes, the people around us can see our strengths more clearly than we can. Their words might be the confirmation you need.

- Ask trusted friends, mentors, or coworkers: *What do you think I'm good at?*

- Listen for patterns in compliments or encouragement you've received.

- Pay attention to when people naturally turn to you for help in a specific area.

4. Experiment and Try New Things

Discovery doesn't happen by waiting—it happens by doing. Many people discover their gifts through new experiences and even trial and error.

- Try volunteering, joining a new group, or tackling a different type of task.

- Be open to stepping outside your comfort zone.

- Notice what activities feel natural or give you a deep sense of satisfaction

5. Pay Attention to Impact and Fulfillment

Your true gift often brings both results and joy. It makes a difference in others' lives—and feels meaningful to you while doing it.

- Where do you consistently see positive outcomes when you act?

- What kind of work or service leaves you feeling energized rather than drained?

- When do you feel most aligned with who you really are?

When Your Gift Doesn't Feel Like a Gift

Not every gift starts with joy or clarity. Sometimes, the very thing you're gifted in feels uncomfortable, unwanted, or even overwhelming. In Scripture, we see this pattern clearly: Moses doubted his ability to lead and speak, even though God had chosen him to deliver a nation. Gideon was called a mighty warrior while hiding in fear, uncertain of his strength or significance. Peter, impulsive and unrefined, probably never imagined he'd become a foundational leader in the early church. Like them, we may discover gifts that surprise us; gifts we didn't ask for, expect, or initially enjoy. But that doesn't make them any less real. Gifts often grow in clarity and appreciation as we walk in obedience and faith.

When Your Gift Feels Insignificant Compared to Others

Many people wrestle with a quiet, internal doubt: "What I have to offer doesn't seem to matter as much as what others bring." Imagine you begin to discover your passion and talent for fashion. In its early, undeveloped state, your creativity may feel small or unimpressive—especially when compared to well-known designers with polished platforms and global recognition. What you bring feels humble, even invisible, while others seem to shine effortlessly, capturing attention with charisma and seemingly extraordinary talent. If left unchecked, this feeling can drain your motivation, steal your joy, and even cloud your sense of purpose. But the truth is: Significance isn't measured by attention; it's measured by authentic contribution. What truly matters is not how loudly your gift is seen, but how faithfully it reflects your unique design. Here are a few points to really keep in mind:

- Value Is Measured by Faithfulness, Not Visibility: The real impact of a gift or talent is not always seen immediately and not always by everyone. In fact, the most life-giving acts are often quiet, consistent, and deeply personal. Think about a caring parent, a thoughtful team member, a neighbor who listens, or the person who quietly holds a group together. These roles rarely get the spotlight, but they hold entire environments in balance.

- What Seems Small May Be Essential: We often confuse flashy with important, but the two are not the same. In any system, whether a company, a family, or a creative project, some roles and contributions are essential, even if they go unnoticed. The structural integrity of a house depends more on its hidden foundation than its paint.

- You Were Designed for Something Specific: Trying to live someone else's strengths will always make you feel like you're not enough. You weren't meant to be a copy—you were meant to be a unique expression of something only you can do. Each person has a different combination of passion, temperament, background, and gifting. When you lean into your own wiring, you contribute in ways no one else can. Comparison drains energy because it focuses on someone else's lane. Confidence grows when you focus on your lane, your contribution, your growth, your direction

- Comparison Can Lead to Self-Sabotage: Comparison can quietly sabotage your growth and purpose. When you start believing that what you bring isn't as valuable as someone else's contribution, it becomes easy to shrink back, to disengage, or to shape yourself into someone you were never meant to be. In chasing another person's expression, you risk losing your own voice and, along with it, the unique impact you were designed to make. This isn't just a personal loss; it's a loss to those around you who need what only you can offer. You don't have to be like someone else to be significant. The world needs both the visionary and the implementer, the loud and the soft, the front-runner and the foundation-layer. Your role may look different, but that doesn't make it any less essential. Diversity in gifts is not a weakness; it's the beauty of how life, community, and purpose are built.

Your gift is not too small. It's exactly what someone needs

Gifted to Serve

Joseph didn't go straight from the dream to the throne. First, he served in Potiphar's house, then he served in prison. This was a hidden season, but it wasn't wasted. God was preparing him.

Discovering your gift is just the beginning—it won't catapult you to the palace overnight. It has to be paired with service. A gift without service is like a seed without soil: full of potential, but incapable of producing fruit. Let's get this straight: You are here to serve. Your gift is not just for success; it's for service. God wired you with a purpose, and your gift is the tool He gave you to fulfill it.

I've seen far too many Christians who are confident in their calling, fully aware of their gift, yet unwilling to serve. They treat service as optional, or worse, beneath them. They misunderstand it as a step backward, a detour, or a mark of low status. But in the Kingdom of God, service is the doorway. So, what role does service play in spiritual growth and purpose?

In today's society, service is often viewed as a weakness. The more power someone gains, the less they serve and the more they expect to be served. Assistants, security, and staff surround celebrities, CEOs, and political leaders, all dedicated to making their lives easier. The world places them on pedestals, where their influence is enjoyed, not exercised for others. This is not how the kingdom worked. In the Kingdom, the more power you have, the greater your call to serve. The more gifted you are, the more responsible you are to use that gift for the benefit of others. The higher God elevates you, the lower you are called to bend in love, humility, and service. In God's Kingdom, greatness is not measured by how many serve you, but by how many you serve faithfully.

Service is not just preparation; it is a sacred process. Before leadership comes servanthood. Before promotion comes humility. Learning to serve teaches you patience, empathy, and discipline, qualities that polish your gift and build your character. Joseph didn't learn administration by reading scrolls in a palace; he learned it by managing another man's household. True greatness is not born in comfort but in the quiet corners where you serve without applause. Service shapes you into someone who can handle success without it corrupting you.

Jesus, the ultimate model of divine authority, did not come to be served but to serve. He said, "For even the Son of Man did not come to be served, but to serve, and to give his life as a ransom for many" (Mark 10:45). Though He was the King of kings, He wrapped a towel around His waist and washed His disciples' feet (John 13:4–5), showing that leadership begins with humility and service. Philippians 2:7-8 says Jesus "made himself nothing by taking the very nature of a servant... he humbled himself by becoming obedient to death, even death on a cross!" His entire ministry, from healing the sick to feeding the multitudes, was rooted in serving others. If Jesus, who had all power, chose to serve first, then service must be the standard and starting point for anyone who desires to lead or build lasting influence.

Service is a requirement to greatness. Just take a moment and think about these verses from the NIV version.

- *"Whoever wants to become great among you must be your servant, and whoever wants to be first must be your slave—just as the Son of Man did not come to be served, but to serve, and to*

> *give his life as a ransom for many." Matthew 20:26–28*

- *"Now that I, your Lord and Teacher, have washed your feet, you also should wash one another's feet. I have set you an example that you should do as I have done for you." John 13:14–15*
- *"Anyone who wants to be first must be the very last, and the servant of all." Mark 9:35*
- *"You, my brothers and sisters, were called to be free. But do not use your freedom to indulge the flesh; rather, serve one another humbly in love." Galatians 5:13*
- *"Each of you should use whatever gift you have received to serve others, as faithful stewards of God's grace in its various forms." 1 Peter 4:10*

You will not find a single great man or woman of God who bypassed the school of service, the lifetime service mandate. From Genesis to Revelation, greatness in the Kingdom is always preceded by humility and service. Let's talk about Joseph.

Before Joseph ever stood before Pharaoh, before he wore royal robes or governed Egypt, he served faithfully in places no one would choose. He was sold into slavery by his own brothers, betrayed by those who should have protected him. Yet even in slavery, he did not become bitter; he became better. In Potiphar's house, Joseph served with such diligence, excellence, and integrity that he was promoted to oversee the entire household. He didn't complain about being a slave; he turned the place of bondage into a platform for stewardship.

Even after being falsely accused and thrown into prison, Joseph did not allow discouragement to make him disengage. Instead, he served again. In a dark, forgotten prison, he became a light, managing responsibilities, caring for fellow inmates, and even interpreting dreams for others while his own remained unfulfilled. He could have shut down. He could have said, "What's the use of serving when I've been forgotten?" But Joseph's service wasn't rooted in his situation; it was rooted in his character. He served like a ruler long before he wore the crown.

Even after Joseph rose to become the second most powerful man in Egypt, he never stopped serving. His promotion didn't make him prideful; it made him even more committed to the purpose behind his position. He wasn't in the palace to be admired; he was there to fulfill an assignment. Joseph understood that leadership is not about being elevated above people but being positioned to serve people at a greater scale.

Pharaoh gave Joseph authority over the land, but Joseph didn't use that power for personal comfort. He immediately got to work creating a national food security system, storing grain, managing resources, and developing a long-term plan to save not just Egypt, but the surrounding nations. When the famine came, he didn't hoard the resources—he distributed them wisely. He negotiated, traded, and preserved life. His role demanded both strategic brilliance and moral integrity, and he offered both in service.

Even more profound was how he served his own family, the very brothers who betrayed him. When they came to Egypt looking for food, he didn't seek revenge—he offered forgiveness, provision, and protection. He gave them land, supplied their needs, and restored the family line that would eventually lead to the birth of Jesus.

Joseph didn't stop being a servant because he was promoted; instead, he served with more impact because of his promotion. And even in power, his heart remained surrendered to God and devoted to people. His life teaches us that actual elevation in God's Kingdom is not the end of service, it's the expansion of it. The higher God lifts you, the more people He calls you to carry.

Let's talk about David. He was anointed king while still a young shepherd boy, tending sheep in obscurity. The oil poured on his head by the prophet Samuel was a divine announcement: "You are chosen. You are called. You are next." Yet, David didn't ascend to the throne the next day; he returned to the field. He went back to the sheep, back to the ordinary, back to serving. But even more humbling was what came next: David entered the palace not as a king but as a servant. He became a musician for King Saul, soothing him with worship when tormenting spirits overwhelmed him (1 Samuel 16:21–23). Later, he became a warrior in Saul's army, faithfully fighting battles for the very man who would grow jealous and seek to kill him.

Despite being hunted, betrayed, and forced to flee for his life, David refused to lift a hand against Saul, even when he had multiple chances. Why? Because David understood that he was Saul's servant. And only servants can be trusted with power. "I will not stretch out my hand against my lord, for he is the Lord's anointed." (1 Samuel 24:10). David's years of serving Saul were shaping him. His time in the palace trained his eyes to see how a kingdom operates. His time in the wilderness taught him to lead men with loyalty and courage. His time in the cave tested his integrity and refined his dependence on God. His service: Trained his heart in honor, even under pressure; sharpened his gift of leadership and strategy through real battles. By the time David finally took the throne, he wasn't just a gifted warrior; he was a man forged in fire, tested by service, and grounded in character.

Even after David became king, he never stopped serving. His position didn't change his posture; he ruled as a servant before God and for the people. While many kings in history used their power to dominate, enrich themselves, or distance themselves from the people, David remained deeply connected to his assignment. He inquired of the Lord constantly, sought God's will before battles, and led with a heart to protect and unify the nation. He wrote psalms to strengthen others, organized worship for the tabernacle, and even prepared the materials for the temple, a house he would never live to see built.

David carried the weight of responsibility with humility. When his people suffered, he fasted. When the judgment came, he repented publicly. When enemies attacked, he went out with his men. David saw the throne as a platform to serve God's purpose. True to the heart of a shepherd, even as king, he continued to feed, lead, and protect the flock entrusted to him. His life is a reminder that in the Kingdom, the higher God elevates you, the deeper He calls you to serve.

Service is the key that unlocks your heart to receive God's blessing and refines the gift He has placed within you. It humbles your ambition, purifies your motives, and prepares your character to carry the weight of your calling. If you skip service, you may receive a gift, but you won't develop the maturity, endurance, or anointing needed to sustain your assignment.

Can You Serve your way to skill? – Application Questions

1. Are you willing to serve even when no one is watching? Do you need a platform or recognition to use your gift, or can you be faithful in hidden places like Joseph in prison or David in the fields?

2. Can you serve someone else's vision before stepping into your own? Are you able to honor and build what belongs to another, like Elisha did for Elijah or Ruth did for Naomi?

3. Do you see service as a privilege or a burden? How do you respond when asked to do tasks that seem minor, repetitive, or behind the scenes?

4. How do you react when your service goes unnoticed? Are you still motivated to serve when you're not thanked, celebrated, or promoted?

5. What is your attitude when the opportunity to serve is inconvenient? Do you serve only when it fits your schedule, or are you willing to sacrifice your comfort for the sake of the Kingdom?

6. Do you associate serving with spiritual maturity or with spiritual weakness? Has culture or pride caused you to see serving as a demotion rather than as the path to greatness?

7. Are you more focused on being used by God publicly or being shaped by God privately? Would you be content if your gift was used to build others quietly, rather than to elevate you visibly?

8. Can you serve with joy even when your gift isn't being fully used? Are you still willing to mop floors or carry chairs if God hasn't opened the door to use your preaching, singing, or leadership yet?

9. Who has God placed around you right now that you can serve? What simple act of service can you do today to meet a need, solve a problem, or bless someone?

10. Do you understand that serving is not a stepping stone, but a lifestyle?

The four wheels of your gift

A car is designed to move forward and backward, but its real purpose is forward motion, getting you to your destination. However, no matter how strong the engine is, if even one wheel is missing, the car isn't going anywhere. You wouldn't trust a vehicle with three wheels to take you across a city, would you? Your gift is like a vehicle, loaded with potential, built for movement. But potential alone isn't enough. Just like a car needs all four wheels to drive, your gift needs four essential components to reach its destination. So let's talk about the four wheels your gift must have to carry you into purpose.

The Wheel of Love

Love is the atmosphere in which every other gift, calling, and act of service is meant to operate. Without love, even the most powerful gift loses its eternal value. As Paul writes in 1 Corinthians 13, we can prophesy, give generously, and even have faith to move mountains, but without love, it profits us nothing. Love is the Kingdom's language, the motive behind its mission, and the measure of its maturity.

True mastery of a gift is not only about skill, but about love, and love is the spirit of true service. Joseph didn't just serve because it was required; he served with care and love, even when he was forgotten, falsely accused, or misunderstood. In Potiphar's house, he went above expectations. In prison, he didn't just manage; he encouraged and helped others. This posture of heart made his service magnetic and unforgettable.

In Genesis 40:6-7, we see a clear picture of this love in action: "When Joseph came to them the next morning, he saw that they were dejected. So, he asked Pharaoh's officials who were in custody with him in his master's house, 'Why do you look so sad today?'" Joseph had every reason to focus on his own pain and injustice, but instead, he noticed the distress of others. It was out of love and compassion that he asked about their well-being. This was servant-hearted leadership. His concern led to an opportunity to use his gift and ultimately positioned him for his breakthrough.

Love transforms skill into ministry. When you serve through love, you stop waiting to be seen, you start seeking who to bless. You listen deeply, help willingly, and stay consistent, even when unnoticed. This was the secret to Joseph's promotion: he served people with excellence and love long before he was rewarded publicly.

This is the mindset Paul echoed in Galatians 5:13: "Through love, serve one another." Whether your gift is in administration, music, speaking, or hospitality, when your heart is anchored in love, your gift becomes irresistible. Love is what gives your work credibility. It makes people remember not just what you did, but how you made them feel. Love in action is what often opens the greatest doors.

Love is a choice, not a feeling. Joseph had every reason to let bitterness, anger, and a thirst for revenge consume him. His journey was marked by deep injustice and pain. Yet Joseph chose love over resentment. His life reflected a continual refusal to allow past wounds to define his present behavior. In Genesis 41:51, when he named his first son Manasseh, he declared, "It is because God has made me forget all my trouble and all my father's household." This wasn't a statement of erasure but of healing. Though his years were filled with sorrow, he chose to act in love for the benefit of others.

Your gift must operate through love. Without love, gifts become noise. Without love, power becomes pride. But when your gift is rooted in love, it reflects the heart of God and becomes a true channel of His grace. *"If I have the gift of prophecy... but have not love, I am nothing."* *(1 Corinthians 13:2).* Love is what makes your service sincere, your leadership safe, and your influence sustainable. So, yes, develop your gift. Refine it. Multiply it. But let love be the reason you use it.

Wealth Principle: Every gift must be developed through consistent use, even when no one is watching. Excellence in obscurity is rehearsal for influence in public. Often, the most effective mastery comes through unpaid service. When Joseph served in Potiphar's house, he wasn't paid—but he was being trained. If you aren't willing to give your gift freely at first, you may not be trusted with it for income later.

The wheel of Excellence

We've just learned that the very purpose of your gift is to serve. In the Kingdom, service isn't optional—it's essential. But let's be clear: not all service is fruitful. Just showing up, going through the motions, or offering your gift carelessly won't produce growth. Service without excellence is a waste of time. If you want your gift to grow, you must commit to serving with excellence.

So what is excellence? Excellence is the decision to bring your best consistently, intentionally, and wholeheartedly. It's not about being perfect. It's not about outperforming others. And it's definitely not about applause. Excellence is doing ordinary things with extraordinary care. As Paul wrote it like this: "Whatever you do, work at it with all your heart, as working for the Lord, not for human masters." (Colossians 3:23). So, what does excellence do for your gift?

Excellence Sharpens the Gift for great success

When you approach your gift with excellence, you're refining it. Excellence stretches you. It pushes you past comfort. It demands more than repetition; it demands growth. It forces you to slow down when something's broken and speed up when it's time to rise. When you choose excellence early in this process, you build a pattern of giving your best. Over time, it creates muscle memory for greatness. And if you don't build that pattern in private, when the big stage comes, it'll for sure expose the gaps.

Excellence Transforms Your Mindset

But this isn't just about skill, it's about who you're becoming in the process. Excellence trains your mind to think differently. It confronts laziness and replaces it with discipline. It removes the "just get by" mentality and replaces it with purpose. It breaks passivity and builds the mindset of a faithful steward. Excellence rewires your brain to embrace challenge as opportunity. It shifts your identity from just being "gifted" to becoming "trustworthy." And that's the kind of person God promotes: gifted and grounded. Excellence grows your character while it matures your gift.

Master Excellence in the Hidden Place

Excellence is rarely built in the spotlight. It's forged in silence in the private decisions when no one's watching. That's where greatness is shaped. Joseph is the perfect example. Yes, he had a divine gift, but what positioned him for greatness was his consistent excellence in the shadows. In Potiphar's house, he managed systems he didn't build. He took care of property he didn't own. And he did it with such diligence that his master entrusted him with everything. In prison, Joseph could've checked out, given up, or grown bitter. Instead, he served. He led. He organized. And again, he was entrusted with more. Every invisible act of faithfulness became visible in due season.

Joseph's excellence in small things created a reputation that echoed far beyond his own life. When Pharaoh needed wisdom, Joseph was the man with the character to lead. Guess where that comes from? From excellent work in shadow. And the fruit of that excellence? When Joseph's family arrived in Egypt, Pharaoh didn't hesitate. He didn't need interviews. He didn't request resumes.

He said: *"If they're connected to Joseph, they're qualified."* Joseph's excellency became a covering over his household. His name became a key that unlocked generational favor. *"The land of Egypt is before you... let them live in the best of the land."* (Genesis 47:6). Remember: Excellence establishes legacy.

The wheel of Integrity

Joseph's rise was also about character. Before God promotes, He proves. And before God can trust you with power, He tests your integrity. Joseph's journey was also a test of his soul. One of his most defining moments came in Potiphar's house. Joseph had a choice: yield to temptation and gain fleeting pleasure or uphold his values and face unjust consequences. He chose to honor God. This was no small decision. Joseph knew no one would find out. But without knowing, he passed the character test by choosing the harder right over the easier wrong.

Building character often demands silent sacrifices and delayed rewards. Joseph's decision to resist Potiphar's wife's advances became a cornerstone of his destiny. What is gained through compromise may offer short-term convenience, but it often leads to long-term regret. In contrast, what is gained through honor becomes a foundation for lasting influence and divine favor.

Integrity is the foundation that sustains the weight of your gift. While your talent may open doors, it's your character, especially your integrity, that determines whether you can stay in the room. Mastering a gift is about becoming the kind of person who can handle the influence, trust, and responsibility that comes with it. Without integrity, your gift becomes dangerous and unsustainable. Integrity keeps you aligned with your purpose, grounded in truth, and faithful in the process, even when no one is watching.

In the quiet seasons, when recognition is scarce and progress feels slow, integrity is what keeps you from cutting corners or compromising your values. Many people fall, not because they lack gifting but because they lack the integrity to carry what the gift produced. That's why David was tested in the wilderness, Joseph in prison, and Daniel in Babylon. God often uses hidden seasons to shape the inner life before He releases public promotion.

Fruit vs. Gift

The Bible talks about gifts and fruits. A gift is given. It is a demonstration of God's grace, not of personal effort. It can be immediate, visible, and even spectacular. However, fruit is different. Fruit must be cultivated through time, pressure, discipline, and in love. It is not bestowed in an instant but grows in obscurity. In Galatians 5:22-23, Paul lists the fruit of the Spirit: love, joy, peace, patience, kindness, goodness, faithfulness, gentleness, and self-control. A person may be admired for their talents, but they are trusted for their character.

Joseph had the remarkable gift of interpreting dreams, but it was his patience, restraint, and unwavering faithfulness that made Pharaoh entrust him with the fate of a nation. Without fruit, even the greatest gift can become a liability.

Character: The Pillar That Holds the Gift

Far too often, people rush to develop their gift but neglect to build their character. Yet without character, a gift becomes unstable like a house with no foundation. I see character as the pillar that holds the weight of your gift. Without it, the very thing meant to elevate you can be the thing that breaks you.

What good is a brilliant financial planner if he's secretly stealing from his clients? What value is an eloquent teacher if he manipulates grades for personal gain? What's the use of a powerful voice, a sharp mind, or creative brilliance if it's all corrupted by pride, dishonesty, or selfish ambition? Your gift might impress people, but only integrity will make you trustworthy.

Jesus said that the wise man builds his house on the rock, not on sand, so that when the storms come, the house stands (Matthew 7:24-27). Character is that rock. It's the solid ground beneath your talent. It's what holds you up when the winds of temptation, pressure, or promotion start to blow.

Whether it's finance, consulting, or the beauty industry, character builds reputation. In a world of shortcuts, transparency becomes your brand. Delivering what you promised, being honest about timelines, staying within ethical boundaries, retains clients, create referrals, and long-term favor.

The wheel of Discipline

Discipline is the daily choice to do what's necessary, not just what's easy. It's the intentional training of your habits, your mind, and your actions in the direction of your calling. It's what takes you from potential to progress, and from gifting to greatness.

Just look at Joseph. He was gifted, yes, but what carried him through betrayal, slavery, and prison wasn't just his gift; it was his consistency, work ethic, and character. From the moment he entered Potiphar's house, Joseph served with excellence, managed responsibilities with care, and did every task as if it mattered.

Genesis 39:3 says, *"His master saw that the Lord was with him and that the Lord gave him success in everything he did."* That kind of fruit doesn't grow by accident; it grows through discipline. When Joseph was falsely imprisoned, his mindset didn't shift. His discipline followed him into the darkness. He kept moving forward with discipline because he knew that Discipline builds trust with God and people. It proves that you're not just gifted, you're dependable.

Proverbs 12:1 puts it plainly: *"If you love learning, you love the discipline that goes with it..."* (MSG). Discipline prepares you for moments you didn't plan. It gets you ready for open doors you didn't expect. Joseph didn't know when his breakthrough would come, but he lived like it could come at any time. That's what discipline does: it keeps you ready.

Discipline can be broken down into two core components: intentionality and consistency.

Intentionality: Growth On Purpose

Intentionality means you don't leave the development of your gift to chance. You grow on purpose. You sharpen your edge with focus.

This looks like:

- Scheduling regular time to practice and sharpen your gift

  → Your gift won't grow just because you pray over it; you have to make time to work on it. Set a rhythm. Build a routine. Put it on your calendar like it matters, because it does.

- Seeking feedback, mentorship, or training to get better

  → God can use others to help shape what He placed inside of you. Excellence invites coaching. You can't reach mastery without input, correction, and people who push you past comfort.

- Facing your weaknesses instead of hiding behind strengths

→ Don't just play to your strong side. Find the weak spots in your skill set and bring them up. Growth comes when you stop avoiding what needs work and confront it with humility.

- Holding yourself accountable not just to outcomes, but to the *how*

  → Excellence isn't just about results—it's about process. Don't just ask, *"Did it work?"* Ask, *"Did I give it my best? Did I honor God in how I did it?"*

Intentionality turns your gift from potential to purpose.

Consistency: Faithfulness Over Time

Consistency separates those who finish from those who only start. It's not always exciting, but it's always effective. Real growth comes from showing up again, and again, and again.

This looks like:

- Practicing even when you're not inspired

  → If you wait for motivation, you'll miss momentum. The best builders keep working when the feelings fade. Passion may spark the fire, but discipline keeps it burning.

- Serving in small, unseen places with the same passion as big ones

→ Your consistency in hidden places proves to God that you're ready for public platforms. Don't despise small rooms. They're training grounds for bigger assignments.

- Building habits that keep your gift sharp and your heart grounded

    → Daily routines protect long-term growth. Whether it's reading, writing, rehearsing, or reflecting, small habits multiply over time. They keep your gift alive and your spirit anchored.

Adding more layers to your gift.

In the Kingdom of God, everything starts as a seed. God rarely gives things in finished form; He provides potential. Whether it's a purpose, a gift, an idea, or an opportunity, what we receive from God often comes in a raw state, requiring us to cultivate, develop, and grow it over time.

Jesus emphasized this truth in the Parable of the Sower (Luke 8:4–15), where He compared the Word of God to a seed sown into various types of soil. The difference wasn't in the seed; it was in the condition of the soil. Some soil rejected it, some received it briefly, and others nurtured it to maturity. Jesus noted that the seed that fell on good ground produced fruit, some thirtyfold, some sixty, and some a hundredfold. In the same way, your gift is a seed, but its growth depends on how you receive, nurture, and protect it. What you do with what God has placed in you will determine whether your gift remains dormant or multiplies.

Every person has been entrusted with a gift, but not everyone realizes it's a seed. Some ignore it. Some bury it. Some recognize it but never take time to develop it intentionally. And even fewer go further to add new layers of skill to it, turning it into a refined tool for impact. For your gift to reach its full impact potential, it must be stirred by passion, stretched through challenge, and strengthened by combining it with other abilities. A gift left untouched remains potential. A gift developed with other abilities becomes power.

When it comes to seeds, a farmer's greatness doesn't come from simply knowing how to identify and sow them. That's only the beginning. To truly reach his full potential, he must learn how to protect the young plants, ensuring they grow to full maturity. He needs to understand timing, seasonal patterns, and how to navigate changing weather conditions. But growth doesn't stop there. To maximize his harvest, he must also become skilled at reaping efficiently, knowing when and how to gather the fruit of his labor. And if he aims to become a thriving agricultural entrepreneur, he must add yet another layer: the ability to market and sell what he produces.

In the beginning, Joseph was simply someone who dreamed. He didn't fully understand the meaning of his dreams, nor did he know how to interpret them with clarity. In fact, when he shared his dreams with his family, it was his brothers and father who interpreted them, not Joseph himself. But over time, he matured in his gift. Through pain, patience, and practice, he eventually mastered the ability to interpret dreams with precision, so much so that he could instantly discern and explain complex prophetic visions. Yet, dream interpretation alone wasn't enough to elevate him to national leadership. To become the second most powerful man in Egypt, Joseph had to add more tools to his gift, like strategic thinking, economic planning, administrative excellence, and emotional intelligence, to lead in a high-pressure political environment. He didn't just grow in revelation; he grew in responsibility, adding layers of wisdom, leadership, and problem-solving that made his gift not only spiritual but practical and scalable for a national crisis.

Layers Added in Potiphar's house.

While serving in Potiphar's house, Joseph entered the first significant training ground for his destiny. Though he had been gifted with vision and favored by God, it was in Potiphar's household that Joseph began to develop the disciplines of leadership, administration, and stewardship. He learned how to manage resources, oversee people, and earn trust through integrity and diligence. Day by day, he was being trained to handle authority not just with competence, but with character. Joseph also learned how to honor leadership, even when the circumstances were unjust, and how to maintain his values in the face of temptation. His resistance to Potiphar's wife was the fruit of a maturing conscience and a growing awareness of God's presence. Through service, responsibility, and testing, Joseph added many layers to his raw gift of vision.

Layers Added in the Prison Season.

Joseph's time in prison looked like punishment, but it was preparation. Though he had already grown in leadership while managing Potiphar's house, prison became the place where his character was deeply tested and his spiritual gifts matured. In that dark and confined place, he developed emotional resilience, deeper trust in God, and relational wisdom. He managed the daily affairs of the prison, proving once again his reliability and earning favor even behind bars. But more significantly, his prophetic gift began to sharpen. He interpreted the dreams of Pharaoh's cupbearer and baker with humility, pointing the glory back to God. Prison became the crucible where his faith was refined, his discernment was tested, and his ability to interpret not just dreams but human behavior was deepened. Joseph learned to wait without losing purpose, to serve without needing applause, and to believe in the promise without seeing results. The dungeon became his classroom, developing in him the wisdom, patience, and humility he would need to stand before kings.

In the table below, we can explore a side-by-side comparison of what Joseph learned in Potiphar's house and the prison. Every stage, whether marked by hardship, waiting, or promotion, carried lessons that sharpened his gift and prepared him for God's greater plan.

Potiphar's House	Prison
Managed within someone else's system	Led without a title or formal authority
Learned excellence and order	Learned empathy and emotional intelligence
Gained favor through administrative skill	Refined spiritual discernment and dream interpretation
Operated under structure and visibility	Developed resilience in hidden, unjust conditions
Built trust through reliable execution	Built influence through quiet service and insight

Every great man of God, at some point, had to add new layers to their gift to increase their influence. They understood a powerful truth: the gift is not the finished product. Here are a few examples:

David – From Worship to Kingdom Leadership

David's journey began in the fields—not with a sword, but with a harp and a heart for God. As a shepherd boy, he developed a deep sense of intimacy with the Lord through worship, often expressing that devotion in song. But David didn't just sing—he began to write. His ability to articulate emotion, prayer, and revelation led to the creation of many of the Psalms, which have become timeless expressions of faith, struggle, and praise. His worship gift matured into a writing gift, shaping the spiritual language of generations.

Yet David didn't stop there. His bold faith in God gave him the courage to face danger—first wild animals, then Goliath, developing his combat skill and trust in God's power. As his responsibilities grew, he layered on leadership, learning to rally men in the wilderness and guide them with vision and loyalty. All of these layers culminated in David becoming a king, where he governed not just with authority but with the heart of a worshipper, the voice of a psalmist, and the mind of a leader. His journey shows that when you keep adding to your gift—whether it's through music, writing, warfare, or wisdom—God will use it to shape a nation and glorify His name.

Paul – From Theologian to Church Architect

Paul began with an intense zeal for Scripture and theology. As a Pharisee, he had deep knowledge, but it was misaligned until his encounter with Jesus. Afterward, he channeled that same passion into preaching, transforming doctrine into life-giving truth for both Jews and Gentiles. He developed his gift further by becoming a writer and teacher, penning letters that would shape Christian doctrine for centuries. He added layers of church planting, pastoral care, and discipleship, raising leaders like Timothy and Titus. Paul even embraced tentmaking, using vocational skills to sustain his mission without burdening others. His gift grew from head knowledge to global impact through intentional layering and service.

T.D. Jakes – From Preacher to Kingdom Builder

T.D. Jakes began with a powerful gift for preaching—a voice marked by passion, insight, and authority. But he didn't stop at the pulpit. Recognizing the broader potential of his gift, he began to add layers that would expand his reach and multiply his influence. He developed into a writer, crafting best-selling books that spoke to the emotional, spiritual, and practical needs of people across the world. From there, he added film and media production, founding T.D. Jake's Enterprises produces movies like Woman Thou Art Loosed and Miracles from Heaven, translating spiritual messages into powerful visual stories. He also became a leadership developer, hosting conferences, training pastors, and mentoring business leaders. Today, Jakes is not only a preacher—he's a cultural voice, thought leader, entrepreneur, and global strategist. His life exemplifies what happens when someone takes their core gift and continues to grow, adapt, and build—layer by layer—for the glory of God.

Priscilla Shirer – From Speaker to Strategic Communicator

Priscilla Shirer began with a strong gift of communication and public speaking, inspired by her father, Dr. Tony Evans. Early on, she used her voice to speak at youth events and women's gatherings. But rather than remaining in one lane, she continued to develop her gift with intentional spiritual depth, committing herself to the study of Scripture and theology. This led her to become a trusted Bible teacher, crafting in-depth Bible studies that have discipled and equipped women around the world. She then added the layer of authorship, writing devotionals, study guides, and books that blend theological accuracy with practical application. Later, she embraced film acting, taking roles in faith-based movies like War Room and Overcomer, expanding her impact beyond the church walls and into mainstream culture. Priscilla Shirer's journey reveals how one gift—when developed with discipline and surrendered to God—can evolve into multiple expressions of Kingdom influence.

Gregory Toussaint – From Preacher to Multinational Kingdom Reformer

Pastor Gregory Toussaint began with a compelling gift of preaching, marked by deep theological insight and bold spiritual authority. But he didn't remain confined to the pulpit—he intentionally layered his calling with tools that would broaden his reach and multiply his impact. A gifted communicator in multiple languages, he expanded his ministry to include radio and media, founding Shekinah FM and creating platforms that reach millions across the Haitian diaspora and beyond. With a sharp intellect, he added academic depth, earning degrees in theology, international law, and accounting, which helped him navigate spiritual, organizational, and societal issues with excellence. He became an author, writing books like Jezebel Unveiled and Nehemiah Arise to equip the Church in spiritual warfare and leadership. Through his role at Tabernacle of Glory, he also emerged as a movement builder, raising leaders, establishing campuses, and influencing the spiritual and civic life of Haitian communities around the world. Gregory Toussaint's journey shows how a man who starts with a gift of preaching can become a global reformer when he faithfully adds layers of wisdom, education, media, and strategic leadership.

Wealth Principle: Discovering to Mastering

True wealth begins when you discover your Divine Edge, your God-given gift that sets you apart. But discovery is only the first step. That gift was never meant for personal glory; it was given so you could serve others with excellence. As you serve, your commitment to intentional practice, consistent discipline, and wholehearted love becomes the key to mastering it. The more you grow in excellence, the more your character will be tested because, without integrity, even the most refined gift becomes a danger rather than a blessing. But if you endure the refining process, stay rooted in love, and submit your gift to God's purposes, He will lead you to add new layers, skills, wisdom, and capacity until your gift multiplies beyond you. The road to wealth in the Kingdom is not accumulation; it's alignment. And alignment comes when your gift, your character, and your calling walk in harmony.

Key Takeaway: After discovering your gift, you must learn it, practice it, master it, and layer it with new skills. Whether you sing, teach, sell, or design, develop stage presence, endurance, communication, and emotional intelligence. A raw gift opens a door, but a refined gift sustains your influence.

Reflection Question: What do others consistently come to you for? Are you sharpening your gift even when no one is watching?

Application Questions:

Gift Discovery & Mastery Questions

1. What unique ability or insight has consistently set you apart from others? " What is your 'divine edge'?
2. How have you used your gift to serve others, especially in unseen or uncelebrated places?
3. What patterns from your childhood or past experiences reveal hints about your core gift?
4. In what ways are you intentionally refining your gift through discipline, learning, or practice?
5. Are there overlooked skills or passions in your life that might be hidden layers of your main gift?
6. How do you respond to seasons of obscurity? Are you still growing when no one is watching?
7. Is your gift currently functioning with the wheels of excellence, integrity, love, and discipline?
8. Can you identify a problem in the world that your gift is uniquely suited to solve?

9. Have mentors, leaders, or peers affirmed your gift in ways you haven't entirely accepted or developed?
10. Are you actively seeking ways to add new layers (e.g., strategy, business, communication) to your primary gift?

JOSEPH, A pathway to wealth

Chapter Three

Solutions Open Thrones

Introduction

Gifts may open doors, but solutions are what keep them open. Joseph's life proves this. From Potiphar's house to Pharaoh's palace, he consistently used his gift to meet real needs. The moment he stood before Pharaoh wasn't about showing off talent; it was about solving a national crisis with wisdom and strategy. This chapter unpacks how your gift, when refined and clearly communicated, becomes a powerful tool for promotion, a key that can unlock thrones.

Life Is About Bringing Solutions to People

Life is not about status, popularity, or talent alone; it's about usefulness. Joseph had been forgotten in prison until Pharaoh had a problem no one could solve. His moment didn't come because he was loud or ambitious; it came because he could bring clarity to confusion. Real influence begins when your presence solves pain points for others.

In every career, calling, or community, people are looking for solutions. Whether it's a business needing innovation, a ministry needing direction, or a family needing healing, those who rise are those who serve by solving. Joseph's story shows us that when you become the answer to a problem, you become indispensable.

Joseph had been solving problems all his life. In Potiphar's house, he managed and improved his master's household, solving administrative and operational challenges with such excellence that he was put in charge of everything. In prison, he helped stabilize the environment and gained the trust of the warden, again managing people and systems effectively. He also interpreted dreams for fellow inmates, offering insight, comfort, and foresight when others were in confusion. Long before he met Pharaoh, Joseph had already proven himself as a consistent problem solver, sharpening his gift through humble service and integrity.

Asking and discovering, "What is my gift?" is a baby step. The giant step is to ask, "Who is my gift solving a problem for?" The bigger the problem, the greater the opportunity to step into your assignment that only his gift could solve. Pharaoh's magicians and wise men failed. It was then that the cupbearer remembered the man who had interpreted his dream and solved his problem. Joseph.

The world isn't moved by your gift alone; it responds to the value you bring to the table. You could be the most talented person alive, but if your gift doesn't solve a problem, you'll likely be overlooked. Throughout history, those who rise and shine are the ones who bring solutions to profound or simple problems, scientific or artistic, political or personal. Heroes are problem solvers. And God has called you to be one of them.

Let's begin with the most undeniable example: Jesus: the Ultimate Problem Solver. From beginning to end, His life was a divine response to human need. People have called Him many names: a prophet, a master teacher, the most compassionate man who ever lived. Others know Him as a friend, a comforter, a healer, a warrior, a Son. And all of these are true, grounded in Scripture. But above all, one truth rises above the rest: He came to solve problems. Every miracle He performed, every word He spoke, and every act of love was a solution to someone's crisis. Jesus didn't just come to impress us with power; He came to serve us with solutions.

Throughout His ministry, Jesus demonstrated His role as a problem solver in every area of life:

- Physical healing: He healed the blind (John 9:1–7), the lame (John 5:1–9), and even raised the dead (John 11:38–44). Each miracle addressed a specific physical condition and restored people to wholeness.

- Emotional and social restoration: Jesus healed the woman with the issue of blood who had suffered for 12 years and was socially isolated (Luke 8:43–48). He also restored the dignity of the woman caught in adultery (John 8:1–11), showing that His solutions addressed shame, guilt, and rejection.

- Provision in crisis: He fed thousands with five loaves and two fish (Matthew 14:13-21) and turned water into wine at a wedding (John 2:1-11). These weren't just miracles—they were timely answers to practical needs.

- Spiritual deliverance: Jesus cast out demons from people like the man in the synagogue (Mark 1:23–26) and the Gerasene demoniac (Mark 5:1–20), freeing them from spiritual bondage.

- Teaching and wisdom: He answered deep moral, spiritual, and theological questions with unmatched clarity and truth (Matthew 22:15-22), often silencing critics and setting captives free with truth.

These are just a few examples among countless others that reveal how Jesus consistently met people at their point of need, bringing not only solutions, but profound transformation. His ministry was never abstract or detached; it was convenient, profoundly personal, and undeniably powerful. Wherever there was pain, confusion, or lack, Jesus showed up with purpose and left behind healing, clarity, and abundance.

Two specific moments in Jesus' ministry always leave me in awe. They proved that no matter how big or small a problem may seem, if it matters to someone, it matters to God. One situation was so simple it might seem almost "unnecessary," while the other was so complex it felt completely unsolvable. And yet, Jesus addressed both with the same compassion and authority. These two examples reveal that as long as it's a real need, whether emotional, physical, or spiritual, it deserves a solution.

The miracle of turning water into wine at the wedding in Cana was not a matter of life and death. No one was dying, starving, or possessed. In fact, the guests had already enjoyed plenty of wine; the celebration was well underway. But the supply ran low, and the potential embarrassment for the bride and groom began to surface. It wasn't a crisis by human standards, but it mattered to them. The disappointment of a ruined wedding, the shame of unmet expectations, and the whispers of guests leaving with a bad impression weighed heavily in the moment. And Jesus showed up. Not because the problem was small or big, but because it was real. This miracle reveals a beautiful truth: God doesn't just care about our survival, He cares about our joy, our dignity, and even the details others might dismiss as "too small."

While some problems are minor and emotional, others are so massive they transcend human ability altogether. The greatest of them all was not just a life-and-death situation; it was an eternal death situation. Humanity was severed entirely from God because of sin. No sacrifice, no ritual, no human effort could restore what was lost. God's justice demanded a price, and no one on earth could pay it. But Jesus did the unthinkable: He stepped in to satisfy divine justice by offering His own life. As Paul writes in Romans 5:7-8, *"Very rarely will anyone die for a righteous person, though for a good person someone might dare to die. But God demonstrates His own love for us in this: While we were still sinners, Christ died for us."* Jesus didn't die for the grateful or the deserving; He died for the guilty, the broken, the rebellious. In doing so, He solved the most significant problem in human history: separation from God. Through His death, He reconnected the entire human race to the possibility of redemption and eternal life

Biblical Examples of People Who Solved Problems and Were Rewarded

- Joseph – He interpreted Pharaoh's dream and provided a solution for a national famine. As a result, he was promoted to second-in-command over all of Egypt (Genesis 41:39–41).

- Daniel – He interpreted King Nebuchadnezzar's dreams and demonstrated unmatched wisdom. This not only saved lives but also earned him a high-ranking position in the Babylonian kingdom (Daniel 2:48).

- David – He solved Israel's military crisis by defeating Goliath. That act of courage brought him into the royal palace, earned him national recognition, and eventually led to kingship (1 Samuel 17).

- Esther – She used wisdom and courage to expose a plot to destroy her people. Because of her solution, the Jewish people were saved, and she was honored by the king (Esther 8:1–2).

- Nehemiah – He solved the problem of Jerusalem's broken walls. His vision, leadership, and planning restored the city and earned him great favor and legacy (Nehemiah 2:17–18; 6:15–16).

Each of these individuals stepped into divine promotion by addressing real problems. Their elevation was not based on ambition but on availability and discernment. They show us that solutions open doors that status alone cannot.

Every gift is a divine solution wrapped in human form. Take the gift of teaching, for example, it's not just about sharing information. It's a response to confusion, ignorance, and misdirection. Where minds are clouded and hearts lack understanding, the teacher shows up to illuminate truth and offer clarity. Likewise, the gift of leadership is God's remedy for chaos and stagnation. When people wander without vision or order, a true leader emerges to cast purpose, bring structure, and move others toward destiny. These aren't random talents; they are targeted tools, designed to meet specific human needs.

Even gifts that seem "non-spiritual" at first glance are God's answers to real-world issues. The gift of creativity, for instance, whether expressed through art, music, or design, brings beauty and emotional healing in a world dulled by stress, despair, and lifelessness. Fashion and styling, when driven by love and discernment, can restore confidence and dignity to those who feel overlooked or unworthy. The one with the gift of hospitality doesn't just serve meals; they mend loneliness, restore belonging, and reflect the Father's welcome. In the Kingdom of God, no gift is wasted because every gift is God's response to a problem someone is praying about.

Matching Your Skill to Real-World Problems

God has equipped every person with fundamental, practical skills, but they have not yet learned how to connect those skills with the pressing needs of the world around them. Identifying the problem your skill solves is the key to discovering your lane of influence and impact.

Joseph was born with the gift of dreams, but that alone wasn't enough to secure his position before kings. Over time, he didn't just dream, he learned to interpret. He deepened his understanding, sharpened his discernment, and eventually combined his spiritual insight with practical leadership. By the time Pharaoh called him, Joseph wasn't just a dreamer; he was a solution carrier. He recognized that his gift, now refined and matured, was the very answer to Pharaoh's crisis and Egypt's survival. And when the moment came, he didn't hesitate; he stepped up with confidence, because preparation had met opportunity.

By recognizing your gift, taking the time to train and refine it, and understanding how it solves real-world problems, you will begin to see overwhelming opportunities unfold before you. What once seemed hidden will now be obvious. Doors will open, not by chance, but because your preparation has created visibility. The world makes room for those who know what they carry and have mastered it.

Here are some examples:

- Teaching or Communication: This skill helps solve problems like ignorance, confusion, or misinformation. Christian educators, coaches, and speakers bring clarity, motivation, and truth into classrooms, pulpits, media, and leadership environments. In many churches and communities, people are expected to speak publicly without ever being taught foundational techniques—such as proper posture, breath control, vocal projection, or body language. If you have the gift of teaching or communication, your ability to coach and equip others can elevate their effectiveness and confidence. Your gift becomes the bridge between raw potential and polished delivery.

- Administration and Organization: This skill addresses chaos, inefficiency, and waste. Churches, non-profits, and businesses thrive when gifted administrators create systems and structures that multiply capacity and reduce stress.

- Creative Arts (Music, Design, Writing): These gifts address emotional, cultural, and spiritual hunger. Whether through worship, storytelling, or visual communication, creatives have the power to heal, inspire, and bridge worlds. One of the most significant cultural challenges is the perceived divide between art and Christianity. Many believers feel unsure about how to embrace their artistic talents within a faith context fully. If you are gifted in creativity, your calling may be to help rebuild that bridge, whether by composing worship music that reflects modern struggles, designing visuals that amplify biblical truths, or writing Bible-based fiction that makes timeless messages accessible to new audiences. Art is not a distraction from the gospel; it can be a vehicle for it. Your creativity may be the key to helping others see God in a new light.

- Hospitality and Care: This gift solves isolation and emotional neglect. A warm home, a meal, a visit, or a listening ear, simple gestures that reflect God's love and restore dignity. But hospitality is not just for personal ministry; it's a powerful bridge in both spiritual and social environments. In churches, hospitable people create welcoming atmospheres for first-time guests, including those who may be exploring faith for the first time. In your community, this gift can open doors for evangelism, mentorship, and healing. Hospitality also plays a vital role in hosting visiting ministers, dignitaries, or political leaders during special events. Whether it's arranging accommodations, managing event logistics, or simply offering heartfelt service, your gift creates a lasting impression of Kingdom excellence. Well-executed hospitality transforms a space from transactional to transformational, making people feel seen, valued, and at home.

- Technical or Digital Skills (Media, IT, Engineering): These talents solve problems related to access, communication, and modernization. In today's technology-driven world, churches and ministries are no exception to the digital revolution. Many churches are transitioning from traditional methods to digital platforms, whether through livestreaming, online giving, digital signage, or church management systems. However, this shift creates a gap for leaders who are unfamiliar with the tools or processes.

If you are skilled in digital media, IT, or engineering, your expertise becomes invaluable. You can help churches modernize their outreach, improve communication, enhance administrative efficiency, and reach broader audiences. From setting up a professional livestream system to developing apps or websites, your contribution can dramatically increase a church's impact. Beyond the church, your skills can serve local businesses, nonprofits, and education centers. The digital world needs Kingdom-minded innovators who can bring excellence, ethics, and vision to tech solutions. This is not just about technical work—it's about transforming how the Gospel is experienced and shared.

- Business Acumen and Entrepreneurship: This skill can powerfully address financial instability, unemployment, and the lack of economic opportunity in both church and community settings. Marketplace leaders who operate with integrity and vision can create jobs, launch ethical ventures, fund missions, and support the infrastructure of Kingdom projects. Many people, especially within the Christian community, have the desire to start a business or become financially independent, but they often don't know where to begin. This creates a massive need for guidance.

If you understand business planning, budgeting, customer service, or sales strategies, you can be the bridge between someone's dream and their first step. Your expertise can help people learn how to craft a business plan, understand market needs, prepare for interviews, and showcase their strengths professionally. You are the solution God placed in your community to unlock others' potential. Beyond profit, your entrepreneurial insight can be used to mentor young adults, build wealth-generating programs in the church, and equip others with financial literacy. Business done with biblical values becomes a vehicle for freedom, stability, and community restoration.

- Hair Care and Personal Grooming: Many people, especially within the Black and African American communities, struggle with understanding how to care for their hair properly. The lack of access to quality information and products often leads to frustration, low confidence, and unnecessary expenses. If your gift lies in hair care, whether it's braiding, styling, product knowledge, or scalp health, you are uniquely positioned to solve a widespread problem. Your skill can educate, uplift, and empower individuals by helping them feel confident, look presentable, and car   e for themselves with dignity. Whether you're teaching a teen how to manage natural curls or helping a professional show up with confidence, your expertise offers both practical help and emotional transformation. This is not just a trade, it's a ministry of care, confidence, and cultural identity.

- Fashion and Clothing Design: Knowing how to dress appropriately, stylishly, and within a reasonable budget is a challenge for many. If your gift is the ability to coordinate colors, styles, and outfits, you are uniquely equipped to solve a significant and practical problem. In your community, there may be young adults preparing for job interviews, individuals needing confidence for public appearances, or church members unsure how to represent themselves with excellence. Your sense of style can help others present themselves with dignity, self-respect, and professionalism. Fashion becomes a tool to boost identity and confidence—and you become the stylist of transformation.

Matching your skill with a problem gives purpose to your passion. It transforms random effort into strategic impact. Don't bury your talent. Pray, observe, and act. Somewhere near you is a problem waiting for the gift God has placed inside you.

Solutions Are the Currency of Promotion

Joseph didn't just interpret the dreams; he offered a plan. He translated divine insight into economic policy. That moved him from prisoner to Prime Minister. "And Pharaoh said to Joseph, 'Since God has made all this known to you... you shall be in charge of my palace.'" (Genesis 41:39–40) Here's the principle: problems are doors in disguise, and people of gifts who carry solutions will always be in demand.

Joseph had every reason to be overlooked. He was an enslaved person, a foreigner, and carried the stain of a false accusation involving Potiphar's wife. In the eyes of Egypt's elite, he had no credentials, no connections, and no political clout. Pharaoh had access to seasoned politicians, magicians, and economists, men who were far more qualified on paper. By every natural standard, Joseph had zero chance of becoming prime minister. But one thing set him apart: he carried the solution to a national crisis. His divine insight and wisdom met a need no one else could fill. This teaches that solutions are the currency of promotion. When you carry what others desperately need, status becomes irrelevant; the door will open not because of who you are, but because of what you solve.

We often think that Jesus received the highest name simply because He is the Son of God. But Philippians 2:7–11 gives us the actual reason He is elevated: "...He humbled Himself by becoming obedient to death, even death on a cross! Therefore, God exalted Him to the highest place and gave Him the name that is above every name." Jesus wasn't exalted merely because of His divine identity; He was exalted because of His radical obedience and ultimate sacrifice. He solved the most significant problem ever faced by humanity: our separation from God. Through His suffering, death, and resurrection, He reconciled humanity back to the Father.

His elevation was the divine reward for solving the "unsolvable", for doing what no one else could.

Getting rewarded for bringing a solution is the rule in the kingdom of God. David is a classic example. His journey to the palace began with a crisis. Crisis! It's a word that stirs fear in the hearts of many; a situation most people try desperately to avoid. To the average person, a crisis means chaos, loss, pressure, or failure. It's uncomfortable. It's unpredictable. It threatens normalcy and exposes weakness. But when Goliath stood mocking the armies of Israel and paralyzing an entire nation with fear, David saw what others called a crisis as a divine opportunity hidden in a dangerous problem. Where others saw a giant too big to fight, David saw a target too big to miss. Armed with faith, a slingshot, and the anointing of God, he brought down what terrified seasoned warriors. That moment changed everything. His victory over Goliath became his entrance into the palace, his introduction to royalty, and the first public confirmation of his destiny. David wasn't promoted because he wanted power; he was elevated because he solved a problem no one else had the courage or faith to face. Goliath wasn't just an enemy; he was a gate. And by defeating him, David unlocked access to a realm that had been closed to shepherds.

Daniel is another excellent example where solution is the currency to promotion. Daniel's rise to influence in Babylon wasn't due to connections, status, or wealth; it was because he consistently brought solutions to impossible problems. When King Nebuchadnezzar had a troubling dream that none of his magicians or advisors could interpret, the entire royal cabinet faced execution. But Daniel stepped forward. Through prayer and divine revelation, he not only interpreted the dream—he described it without even being told what it was. This display of supernatural insight saved lives and astonished the king. Immediately, Daniel was promoted to a high position, given great wealth, authority over the entire province of Babylon, and made chief over all the wise men (Daniel 2:48). His gift didn't just solve a crisis; it opened doors of power, provision, and influence.

Remember, you are here to bring a solution, and you will be rewarded for that.

Real-Life Examples of People Who Solved Problems and Were Elevated

In every generation, elevation and wealth often flow to those who solve meaningful problems. These individuals didn't chase money; they chased purpose, and money followed solutions.

- Elon Musk, troubled by the environmental crisis and global dependency on fossil fuels, didn't just talk about change—he engineered it. Through Tesla, he revolutionized electric vehicles, battery storage, and clean energy innovation. Today, he is one of the wealthiest men on earth, with an estimated net worth of $190–220 billion. His influence spans space exploration, AI, and global infrastructure, but it all began with solving a global energy problem.

- Oprah Winfrey rose from a traumatic and poverty-stricken childhood to build a media empire that brought healing, conversation, and empowerment to millions. By creating a platform that addressed emotional, social, and cultural wounds, she became a trusted voice in households worldwide. Her talk show alone earned her hundreds of millions, and her total net worth is now estimated at $2.8 billion. Her influence proves that emotional and cultural solutions have economic power.

- Dr. Ben Carson, once a struggling student raised by a single mother in poverty, rose to become one of the world's most respected neurosurgeons. His groundbreaking surgery—successfully separating conjoined twins—placed him at the top of the medical world. Though not a billionaire, Carson earned millions in both medicine and later through books, speaking engagements, and public service. His life demonstrates that skillful problem-solving builds lasting honor, reputation, and open doors beyond your field.

- Sara Blakely, frustrated by uncomfortable undergarments, created Spanx with $5,000 in savings and no background in fashion. Her innovation was simple but powerful: solve a real problem for real women. Spanx exploded globally, making her the youngest self-made female billionaire, with a peak net worth of approximately $1.2 billion. Her story is proof that even everyday problems can birth extraordinary wealth when met with creativity and courage.

- Malala Yousafzai, after surviving a brutal attack for advocating girls' education, turned her pain into global advocacy. Though not driven by profit, Malala has earned millions through speaking engagements, book deals (like I Am Malala), and the Nobel Peace Prize. Her net worth is estimated between $2 and $3 million, and she has used her influence to fund schools and educational initiatives across the world. Her story shows that even advocacy can create value when rooted in solving injustice.

These individuals came from different backgrounds: tech, media, medicine, fashion, activism, but they share one thing in common: they saw a problem, developed a solution, and wealth followed. In both biblical and modern times, the formula remains the same: solutions are magnets for both promotion and provision.

Personal Reflection: I discovered that teaching was more than just something I enjoyed—it was a gift, a divine edge. However, for a while, it didn't feel like I was using that gift to solve any real problem. I loved explaining concepts and helping others learn, but I did it randomly and without direction.

During my time in high school and college, I observed something that changed everything. There were many talented, credentialed teachers, some with doctoral degrees, who deeply understood their subjects. Yet, despite their expertise, students constantly struggled. Complaints were common. Many students struggled to understand the material and see its connection to real life. As a result, large numbers were failing or giving up on subjects altogether.

That's when I realized what my gift was really for. My ability to simplify complex ideas and connect them to practical, everyday examples allowed me to bridge that gap. I could make complex topics not only understandable but also relatable. Slowly, I began to see the impact. Students started learning. They started passing. They started believing in themselves. That's when I truly realized that teaching wasn't just my passion, but my calling to solve a real problem in real lives.

How to start attracting provision

You've discovered your gift, and you didn't stop there. You invested the time to sharpen it, to grow in it, and to understand it. The timeline may have been different from others because development is never one-size-fits-all. But through that process, something powerful happened: you uncovered the purpose behind your ability. You now know why you carry this gift and what problem you were born to solve. This is no longer about talent; it's about assignment. And now, the season of preparation has done its work. It's time to emerge. Time to let your gift speak. The world doesn't just need your potential, it requires the solution you carry and it's your responsibility to show up and serve.

Strategy 1 – Selling for free

Joseph served Potiphar with excellence and love, expecting no reward in return. He worked faithfully in prison, managing duties and interpreting dreams without pay or personal benefit. But this wasn't because Joseph lacked confidence in his gift; it was a divine strategy at work. Serving for free is a powerful act of preparation.

Too many people today want to start with a price tag before they've built credibility. They demand payment or recognition before they've developed proof. But Joseph shows us a higher way: you must become the service before you sell the service. What does that even mean to become the service? You become the service when you embody the value you're offering before trying to convince others to buy into it. If you're selling leadership coaching, you must first lead yourself well. If you're offering healing or encouragement, you must first walk in emotional wholeness. If you're promoting excellence, your own life must reflect excellence. In short, authenticity is the foundation of credibility. The world can sense when someone is simply marketing versus when someone is living their message. When you become the service, it flows naturally—you speak from experience, lead by example, and attract trust.

When you first start, you must sell your ability for three.

Here are just a few benefits of offering your service before charging for it:

1. Perfecting your gift – Offering your gift freely places you in real-life conditions where theory meets experience. Without the pressure of a price tag, you have the freedom to explore, stretch, and experiment. Every opportunity becomes a live workshop—where feedback is honest, challenges are diverse, and your raw talent is constantly sharpened. You're not just rehearsing; you're refining. In these moments, your gift evolves from potential to precision. You gain insight into what works, what doesn't, and how to deliver excellence consistently. Freely serving becomes your training ground, where what was once instinct becomes skill, and what was once talent becomes trusted expertise.

2. Making necessary corrections – When you serve without charging, you enter a grace-filled space where failure is not fatal, it's formative. You're free to make mistakes, receive feedback, and pivot quickly without the fear of disappointing paying clients. In this environment, your communication, timing, and execution are tested and adjusted in real time. It's where you can fall forward without shame, transforming clumsy beginnings into lasting mastery. The freedom to make corrections in this phase is priceless. It builds muscle memory, emotional intelligence, and confidence. Every misstep becomes a mentor, helping you avoid costly errors later and

ensuring you deliver with excellence when it truly counts

3. Clarifying Your Market Fit – In the early stages, most people try to serve everyone, casting a wide net and hoping something sticks. But serving freely gives you room to experiment without financial pressure. As you engage different audiences, needs, and scenarios, patterns begin to emerge. You start to see where your gift brings the most impact, who resonates with your message, and what problems you're best equipped to solve. This clarity is gold. It sharpens your focus, hones your message, and reveals your proper niche. Eventually, you stop chasing everyone and start attracting the right ones.

4. Building a trusted network – When you give without asking, you sow seeds that money can't buy: trust, respect, and relational capital. Serving selflessly showcases not just your skill, but your character. People experience your heart, your consistency, and your excellence firsthand. That kind of impact builds something deeper than followers—it builds advocates. Relationships born of generosity often open doors you couldn't have knocked on alone: speaking invitations, referrals, partnerships, and clients willing to pay premium prices—not just for your work, but for who you've proven yourself to be. Trust travels further than talent. Providing free service with

excellence becomes a powerful magnet for long-term opportunities.

5. Developing Emotional Resilience Serving freely isn't just about sharpening your gift; it's about strengthening your soul. When there's no applause, no paycheck, and no immediate reward, your inner world is tested. Can you still show up with excellence? Can you serve without being seen? This process purifies your motives and builds emotional maturity. You learn to manage frustration, delay gratification, and navigate criticism without falling apart. You gain discernment—when to speak, when to be silent, when to push forward, and when to rest. These invisible lessons produce visible fruit: humility, patience, empathy, and self-control. Before God entrusts you with public influence, He shapes your private integrity. Emotional resilience isn't optional—it's a requirement for sustained success and spiritual leadership.

Joseph's early generosity created the kind of credibility that made Pharaoh listen. Genesis 41:9–13 reveals how the cupbearer remembered Joseph, not because Joseph demanded recognition, but because of the unforgettable quality of his service. Joseph had interpreted the cupbearer's dream with precision. He offered insight, compassion, and excellence purely out of his calling. That moment of unpaid service became the seed of future promotion.

When the time came for Pharaoh to find a solution, it wasn't Joseph's résumé that brought him forward; it was a personal testimony from someone he once helped. The cupbearer had experienced Joseph's integrity, wisdom, and generosity firsthand. That memory was so strong, so impactful, that he didn't hesitate to recommend Joseph to the king. Can you imagine how history might have changed if Joseph had kept his gift to himself?

This is the power of serving freely in alignment with Kingdom purpose. What you do in secret can speak loudly in rooms you've never entered. Don't underestimate the season of serving without payment; it's not just preparation; you are positioning yourself for future influence and access.

Personal Reflection: There was a time when I found myself wrestling with the idea of offering my gift freely. I knew I had something valuable to share, but the thought of giving without compensation felt like a step backward. Still, deep down, I sensed God calling me to serve first— to focus on impact, not income. As I began to teach, mentor, and contribute without expecting anything in return, I noticed something powerful. My confidence grew. My skills sharpened. More importantly, people began to trust me. Opportunities I never imagined started to unfold—not because I pushed for payment, but because I planted seeds of service. Looking back, I see that season not as a delay, but as divine training. I wasn't just preparing others; I was being prepared myself.

Wealth Principle Takeaway: Wealth in the Kingdom doesn't begin with pricing your gift—it starts with proving it through love, excellence, and faithful service. When you serve without expecting payment, you build something far more valuable than money: you build credibility, trust, and legacy. This invisible capital becomes the foundation for a visible increase. Joseph didn't pursue promotion; he pursued excellence and service, and promotion found him.

Strategy 2 - Persuasive Communication

The next crucial step is learning how to communicate it with clarity and conviction. Excellent communication isn't manipulation; it's the ability to clearly articulate the value you bring in a way that connects with real needs. It's about framing your message, sharing your story, and demonstrating the transformation your gift offers.

Joseph exemplifies this principle masterfully in Genesis 41. When Pharaoh summoned him to interpret a troubling dream, he said, *"I had a dream, and no one can interpret it. But I have heard it said of you that when you hear a dream, you can interpret it"* (v. 15). Some people would leap at the chance to showcase their talent, but not Joseph. Instead, he replies, *"I cannot do it... but God will give Pharaoh the answer he desires"* (v. 16). This was strategic positioning. Joseph immediately shifted the focus from his personal ability to God's divine wisdom, anchoring his gift in purpose. In doing so, he elevated the conversation from talent to spiritual authority. At a time when divine insight was deeply respected, even by pagan kings, Joseph captured Pharaoh's attention by presenting himself not just as a gifted man, but as a vessel of heaven's solution. This is persuasive communication at its best: humility without hesitation, clarity without self-promotion, and influence rooted in the fear of God.

From verses 17 to 24, Pharaoh shares his dream in detail. He doesn't explicitly ask for a solution; he expresses concern. But Joseph, discerning the more profound need, offers more than interpretation. He understands that insight alone won't solve the crisis; a strategy is required. Without being prompted, Joseph transitions in verse 33 into a bold proposal: a comprehensive, long-term economic plan to preserve Egypt through the coming famine.

This moment reveals Joseph's brilliance not just as an interpreter but as a visionary leader. His communication was clear, confident, and practical. He not only named the problem, but he also outlined a solution that was timely, executable, and wise. The result? Pharaoh and his officials were so impressed that Joseph was instantly promoted to second-in-command (Genesis 41:39–41).

Joseph's gift opened the door, but his ability to communicate positioned him in the palace. He didn't boast or oversell, he aligned his words with the need and presented his solution as the answer Pharaoh didn't know he was looking for.

This story teaches us that mastering your gift is only half the equation. Knowing how to communicate it effectively, especially in critical moments, is what truly brings elevation. Whether in a boardroom, a pulpit, an interview, or a digital platform, your ability to clearly express your value builds trust, expands influence, and attracts opportunities.

Knowing how to communicate your gift is essential to unlocking opportunities. You can be incredibly talented or deeply anointed, but if you can't clearly and confidently express the value you bring, people won't recognize or respond to it. In many cases, doors remain closed not due to lack of skill but lack of clarity. In a noisy world, those who communicate with purpose stand out. Whether it's in a conversation, a pitch, a platform, or an online presence, how you speak determines how your gift is perceived and whether others trust, follow, or invest in you. In today's digital landscape, platforms like social media, YouTube, podcasts, and email are modern stages for your message. And with the rise of AI tools like ChatGPT, Canva AI, and marketing automations, learning to communicate and to leverage technology effectively is no longer optional. It's the key to multiplying your reach, scaling your impact, and staying relevant in a rapidly evolving world.

Strategy 3 - Strategic Positioning

Joseph didn't just interpret Pharaoh's dream—he used that insight to position Egypt as the most essential and irreplaceable nation in the region. By storing grain during the years of abundance, he transformed Egypt into the only reliable source of food during the famine. When the crisis hit, every surrounding nation came to Egypt—not just for help, but for survival. This wasn't accidental; it was strategic. Joseph understood the power of becoming needed, not just known. He positioned the nation as the solution, and in doing so, he made himself the most valuable man in the empire. People didn't come looking for Joseph—they came looking for grain. But because Joseph controlled the grain, he became the man no one could ignore. That's the power of strategic positioning: becoming so aligned with the solution that people can't get what they need without coming through you.

Joseph's success wasn't just about his gift—it was about his foresight. He knew what was coming and positioned himself accordingly. After interpreting Pharaoh's dream, Joseph didn't just stop at revelation—he anticipated the future and developed a plan to capitalize on it. He saw the famine before it arrived and used the years of abundance to create systems that would make Egypt indispensable. This is a powerful strategy for every gifted person: it's not enough to be reactive—you must be prophetic in how you prepare. If you can't see what's ahead, you'll miss your moment. Gifting without foresight will keep you busy but not effective. As a visionary leader, you must learn to sense opportunity, read patterns, study environments, and prepare for what others are ignoring. Joseph didn't wait for a crisis—he positioned himself to own the solution before the crisis came, and that's what made him essential. Likewise, if you want to rise in influence, you must not only carry a gift—you must know how to read the times and move with wisdom.

These individuals became prosperous and wealthy because they saw the wave coming and positioned themselves for it, while others remained on the sidelines, unprepared and unaware.

- Jeff Bezos – Founder of Amazon: Bezos anticipated the explosion of online shopping before it became mainstream. He started Amazon in 1994 as an online bookstore, but from the beginning, he had a vision for it to become "the everything store." While others focused on short-term retail wins, Bezos built long-term infrastructure, including warehouses, logistics, and cloud services (AWS). He positioned Amazon not just to sell—but to dominate future global commerce. Today, Amazon is a multi-trillion-dollar empire

- Khaby Lame – TikTok Star: Khaby became famous by posting silent reaction videos to overly complicated "life hacks." He didn't speak a word—but his timing, facial expressions, and message were universal. At a time when TikTok was exploding, Khaby strategically positioned himself with humor, simplicity, and relatability. He filled a global content gap without needing language—and became one of the most followed creators on the platform. His simplicity became his strategy

- Tabitha Brown – Actress & Wellness Influencer: Tabitha went viral on TikTok for her calming voice, warm energy, and delicious vegan recipes. She entered the platform with authenticity and consistency, sharing content that made people feel better during the pandemic. Her brand grew rapidly because she was strategically positioned where people were hungry for comfort and positivity. Now, she has TV shows, books, and brand deals—all because she discerned the moment and showed up with value

Knowing how to position yourself also means knowing how to recognize and respond to a crisis. Every crisis carries hidden opportunities, doors that only open for those discerning enough to see beyond the chaos. While others panic or retreat, those with foresight and strategy rise. Crises are opportunities in disguise, waiting for someone bold enough to bring a solution. Just as Joseph leveraged famine to elevate Egypt, you can use disruption to step into your destiny. Strategic positioning means you don't just survive storms, you use them to sail farther

- Content Creators & Coaches – Post-COVID Digital Boom: Many people lost jobs during COVID and started building online businesses, podcasts, coaching brands, or digital ministries. The crisis gave rise to a new wave of entrepreneurs who leveraged social media and technology to serve, teach, and lead. Some became six- and seven-figure earners from their living rooms.

- Zoom – COVID-19 Pandemic: Before 2020, Zoom was just another video conferencing tool.

But when the pandemic hit and people were forced to work, learn, and worship from home, Zoom became the default communication platform. The company's value skyrocketed, making it one of the biggest tech winners of the COVID era

- Airbnb – Born from the 2008 Financial Crisis: The global recession forced many people to find new ways to earn income. Airbnb's founders offered air mattresses in their apartment to travelers looking for cheaper accommodations, and the idea took off. What started as a crisis-driven hustle became a billion-dollar hospitality company, changing the way we travel.

Here are a few key principles you should consider to position yourself strategically

- Embrace Technology Early. We're in a digital era where AI, automation, and digital platforms are shaping the future. Don't resist it—leverage it. Tools like ChatGPT, Canva AI, and digital courses can help you scale faster, reach more people, and save time. Those who adopt new tools early often gain the most significant advantage.

- Opportunities often hide in the gaps: Ask yourself: What's frustrating people? What could be done better? What's not being said, offered, or solved? If you can fill that gap with excellence, people will pay for it. Sara Blakely built Spanx by solving a clothing problem most people ignored simply by identifying what was missing.

- Study Trends and Patterns. One of the best ways to identify opportunities is by paying attention to what's changing. Follow industry news, social shifts, and technological developments. Trends always leave clues. Instead of reacting late, position yourself early where attention and demand are going. People who studied the rise of remote work, digital products, or short-form content were able to ride the wave while others were still watching.

- Be curious and ask questions. People who consistently ask questions often uncover possibilities others miss. Curiosity keeps you alert, engaged, and aware of hidden problems that your gift might be able to solve. Strategic thinkers don't wait for answers to come to them; they ask, explore, and investigate. When you're curious, you naturally dig deeper, connect ideas, and position yourself as a solutionist. The most innovative businesses and impactful ministries are often built not from having all the answers, but from asking the right questions.

Strategy 4 - Learn to take risks

Risk, by definition, is the willingness to step into uncertainty with the possibility of loss, but also the potential for gain. It is the intentional act of leaving comfort zones in pursuit of growth, purpose, or calling. Every great move forward in scripture and history involved someone stepping into the unknown with faith, strategy, and courage. Risk is the bridge between where you are and where your calling is waiting.

Joseph's entire journey was marked by strategic risk. When he interpreted Pharaoh's dreams, he did more than explain symbols; he proposed a national strategy to save Egypt from famine. That took extraordinary boldness. Up to that point, all Joseph had ever managed were Potiphar's household and the operations within a prison, both confined and controlled environments. Suddenly, he was offered the monumental responsibility of managing an entire nation and leading through fourteen critical years. He could have backed away, claiming the task was beyond him, or he could have chosen the safer path of remaining behind the scenes. But Joseph took a calculated risk, recognizing that his years of hidden preparation had uniquely equipped him. He drew on every lesson from his past, every moment of faithful service, and stepped forward in confidence. His decision to rise to the challenge wasn't arrogance; it was alignment with purpose, grounded in faith and seasoned by discipline (Genesis 41:33-36).

Risk is not gambling. It's a calculated step built on preparation, prayer, and perspective. Esther took a risk when she approached the king without being summoned. David took a risk when he faced Goliath. Peter took a risk when he stepped out of the boat. Ruth left her homeland and chose a new people and God. Her decision to risk her future by following Naomi led her to

Boaz and into the lineage of Christ. In every case, God met the person in motion, not passivity.

People who change the world are not those who play it safe; They are those who act boldly. Taking a risk doesn't mean you won't feel fear; it means you refuse to let fear make your decisions. This journey takes time, and though it may not always feel glamorous, it's a sacred preparation for something greater. Along the way, you'll face uncertainty, and fear will try to whisper that you're not ready. But fear, while a natural emotion, must be mastered, not obeyed. It's meant to alert you, not to paralyze you. Growth never happens in comfort zones. As you commit to the process, sharpen your skill, and move with courage, you'll find that the very fear that once held you back becomes fuel for boldness. Keep moving. The reward is on the other side of risk.

Start with small risks: initiate a conversation, launch that idea, share your solution. The more you stretch your courage muscle, the more prepared you'll be for greater leaps.

"Whoever watches the wind will not plant; whoever looks at the clouds will not reap." —Ecclesiastes 11:4 - "Faith without works is dead." —James 2:26

Wealth Principle:

Taking calculated risks is essential for expanding influence, creating value, and unlocking new opportunities. Every breakthrough—spiritually or financially—requires a step of faith. Playing it safe may preserve comfort, but rarely multiplies purpose. Those who build generational wealth and legacy often do so by moving forward when others hesitate. Like Joseph, risk tied to preparation becomes a divine strategy for elevation.

Reflection Questions: Developing Your Problem-Solving Ability

1. What practical problems do people around you consistently face?
2. What challenges do people usually come to you for help with?
3. Which of your skills or gifts naturally bring relief, clarity, or transformation to others?
4. Have you identified a gap in your church, community, or industry that your gift could help fill?
5. Are you willing to offer your gift in service before demanding compensation?
6. How can you improve or deepen your skill so you solve that problem more effectively?
7. Who are a few people or groups that would benefit immediately if you activated your gift today?
8. What has been stopping you from stepping forward as a solution?

These questions are not just for journaling, they're for clarity. Your next level of impact begins when you match your gift with someone's need.

Chapter Four

Expand Your Gift

Introduction

Joseph knew that a gift alone isn't enough to create a lasting impact. It must be activated, aligned, and supported to reach its full potential. This chapter reveals why your gift needs more than passion; it needs partnership, structure, and investment. When your gift is given in the right environment, it multiplies, impacts, and outlives you.

"You can't multiply what you don't manage. You can't elevate what you don't systemize." Inspired by the life of Joseph

"Go to the ant, you sluggard; consider its ways and be wise... it stores its provisions in summer and gathers its food at harvest."— Proverbs 6:6 8 (NIV)

Joseph's journey teaches us that elevation is not just about being gifted; it's about building systems that multiply the gift. His insight from God positioned him to solve a national crisis, but what truly changed the game was how he scaled that gift to impact an entire nation and beyond.

Joseph's refined gifts and faithful service have brought him before Pharaoh, and with that, his first reward was massive. Practically overnight, he stepped into a position of wealth, authority, and influence. His "business", his calling, and leadership capacity were now officially operating at a national level.

However, with such elevation comes a choice: hoard power or expand influence. Many people in leadership fall into the trap of concentrating authority around themselves. Likewise, many business owners limit growth because they try to control everything alone, driven by fear or a small vision. In the Christian world, many enterprises remain underdeveloped, not due to a lack of anointing, but rather a lack of an expansion mindset.

Joseph chose differently. He embraced delegation. He built systems. He empowered others. His expansion strategy was essential. And it's a Kingdom principle we must all adopt if we want our gifts to multiply and leave a lasting impact.

Expand through leaders

One of the fastest and most effective ways to grow is through people. Multiplication is a universal principle: no great mission is accomplished alone. Even Jesus, though fully divine, did not try to reach every city or region by Himself. He recognized the importance of growth through people. He chose 12 disciples, later appointed 70 more, and after Pentecost, 3,000 were added in a single day—immediately multiplying the mission by reaching others.

We must adopt the same model. Because we cannot be everywhere at once, we must empower others to carry the vision. Delegation is multiplication. The more people you equip, the greater your gift's impact across regions, cultures, and generations.

"Joseph stored up huge quantities of grain, like the sand of the sea..." — Genesis 41:49 One man couldn't do that alone. It required systems, people, and strategy. Likewise, there are levels of wealth, influence, and impact we'll never reach if we rely solely on our individual effort. We all have 24 hours—but if you train 10 people to operate in your gift, you now have 240 hours working toward your mission.

Joseph understood this. In Genesis 41:34, he advised Pharaoh to appoint commissioners to oversee grain collection. This wasn't a suggestion for convenience—it was a strategy for scalability. Those appointed leaders became an extension of Joseph's vision, faithfully executing the system he designed.

In verse 46, we read that Joseph "traveled throughout Egypt." This wasn't sightseeing—it was strategic oversight. He was inspecting, training, and equipping others. His influence expanded because he didn't try to do everything himself—he multiplied his insight through people. Joseph didn't need helpers; he needed leaders. Leaders who could carry the weight of responsibility with the same excellence and clarity he carried. That's why he traveled—not to micromanage, but to mentor. The more he poured into others, the more his gift expanded without burnout.

This principle begins with God Himself. In Genesis 1:26, God said, *"Let us make mankind in our image, in our likeness, so that they may rule..."* God knew that rulership requires shared capacity. You cannot reign like God if you are not shaped like God. Being made in His image means being entrusted with His nature, creativity, and authority. Likewise, when we raise others in our likeness—imparting our values, vision, and skill—we are not just delegating, we are replicating.

Jesus modeled this flawlessly. He didn't just gather followers—He built leaders. He trained His disciples so thoroughly that He transferred His mindset, authority, and power to them. In John 14:12, He said, *"Whoever believes in me will do the works I have been doing, and they will do even greater things..."* This wasn't just a promise; it was the fruit of intentional discipleship. Jesus didn't just lead—He reproduced Himself. That's the model for anyone who desires to multiply their influence, expand their reach, and scale their gift beyond personal limitations.

"If you want to go fast, go alone. If you want to go far, go together." — African Proverb

"And the things you have heard me say in the presence of many witnesses entrust to reliable people who will also be qualified to teach others." — 2 Timothy 2:2 (NIV)

"Two are better than one, because they have a good return for their labor." — Ecclesiastes 4:9 (NIV)

Duplicating yourself will provide you with these benefits

- Exponential growth: When you train and empower others to operate at your level, growth shifts from linear to exponential. Many assume that if one person can accomplish ten tasks, two people will do twenty. But actual multiplication creates synergy, not just division of labor. Imagine you have four heavy tables to move from point A to point B. Alone, you might need four minutes, moving one at a time. But if you have a trained partner, both of you can carry two tables simultaneously and complete the job in just two minutes. The time is cut in half, and the output doubles. Now imagine a third person joins, and the system becomes even more efficient. This is the power of empowered collaboration; what once took great effort becomes easier, faster, and more impactful. It's not just about adding hands, it's about multiplying effectiveness.

- From doer to leader. One of the most significant benefits of multiplying yourself is the ability to redeem your time and redirect your energy. When you're the only one doing the work, your time becomes a ceiling—your own strength, hours, and capacity limit you. But when you train and empower others to carry part of the load, you free yourself from the constant grind of execution. You stop being just the operator and start functioning as the orchestrator.

This shift allows you to zoom out and see the bigger picture. You gain space to think strategically, explore new ideas, solve problems creatively, and lead with vision. Rather than being consumed with the day-to-day, you're now positioned to anticipate challenges, identify opportunities, and make decisions that move the entire mission forward.

Consider Moses in Exodus 18: he was exhausting himself by handling every case among the Israelites. But when Jethro advised him to appoint capable leaders over groups of people, Moses was freed to focus on what only *he* could do—hearing from God, setting direction, and leading the nation.

- Team Momentum and Resilience. When you surround yourself with well-trained, like-minded individuals, you don't just increase capacity, you build a culture of motivation and resilience. In a strong team, momentum is contagious. When one person feels discouraged, another's determination can lift the atmosphere. You push each other forward, celebrate each other's wins, and carry each other through challenges. Together, you become more resilient, not because trials disappear, but because you're no longer facing them alone. Well-equipped teams are like a braided cord: each strand reinforces the others. This kind of unity doesn't just help you endure hardship; it empowers you to overcome it with strength, courage, and renewed purpose. The journey becomes less about survival and more about shared growth and victory.

When you build a team like this, you also multiply income, opportunities, and wealth. When your team can think, serve, and execute at your level of excellence, you're able to reach more people without sacrificing quality. Each member becomes a multiplier, able to spot and seize opportunities you might never see alone. And as this culture compounds, your business becomes a money-making machine, fueled by shared vision, high standards, and a united drive. With you leading and empowering from within, growth becomes exponential.

Expand through partners

It's essential to build leaders around you who think, act, and move under your leadership—aligned with your vision and the mantle of your gift. These are the people who help carry the mission forward with consistency and conviction. However, not everyone in your circle will serve as a direct leader under you. Some will be partners, and their role is just as vital. A partner may not be part of your core team, but they are a strategic channel through which your gift or product gains access, visibility, and influence. Partners are connectors, people with high-value networks who can open doors you couldn't reach alone.

In Joseph's case, Pharaoh was a key partner; he provided the platform for Joseph's gift to be activated and recognized at a national level. Likewise, the governors and tribal leaders across the surrounding nations acted as distribution channels, allowing Egypt's grain to be sold far beyond its borders. These partnerships expanded Joseph's reach and turned local provision into regional dominance. In the same way, your gift needs both loyal leaders and strategic partners—those who walk with you, and those who position you.

What does that look like for your gift:

1. Platform Partners

    Who they are: People or organizations who give you access to their audience or platform

Why they matter: They increase visibility and credibility by putting your gift in front of new crowds

Examples:

- o A podcast host who interviews you

- o A church or conference that invites you to speak

- o A blog, media outlet, or influencer who features your content

2. Distribution Partners

Who they are: Individuals or systems that help circulate your product, book, course, or message

Why they matter: They get your gift into more hands and generate revenue

Examples:

- o Bookstores or online retailers (for example Amazon, Shopify, church bookstores)

- o Affiliate marketers and brand ambassadors

- o Coaches or consultants who include your resource in their offerings

3. Kingdom Partners

Who they are: Fellow ministers, creators, or visionaries aligned spiritually and missionally

Why they matter: They walk in unity, pray with you, and advance the Kingdom alongside you

Examples:

- A like-minded author you co-host a summit with

- A ministry that collaborates on outreach projects

- A mentor who provides spiritual covering

Expand through Systems

Without systems, blessings can quickly turn into burdens. Joseph's most significant contribution to Egypt wasn't just interpreting Pharaoh's dream; it was the creation of a strategic, long-term system that would protect the nation through seven years of famine. He didn't just prophesy the problem; he engineered the solution.

What is a System?

A system is a repeatable and organized process that ensures consistency, efficiency, and scalability. It takes your unique approach and turns it into a structure that others can follow. Systems allow your gift, your values, and your methods to operate even when you're not present.

Genesis 41 reveals how Joseph established granaries, distribution plans, supply routes, and oversight structures. He implemented a 20% grain collection policy and ensured that food was stored in every city. This was not just about storage; it was about creating self-sufficiency across the nation. Each city was equipped to manage its own supply without relying entirely on the central government. In addition to this decentralized model, Joseph put in place an inspection and verification system, which is one of the reasons he traveled throughout Egypt (Genesis 41:46). He ensured accountability, consistency, and readiness at every level. These were components of a well-designed system that transformed Egypt into a resilient and prosperous economy. When the famine struck, Egypt not only survived, but it also became a global supplier of food. Egypt became the go-to country.

Systems turn revelation into preservation. They secure the blessing God gives. Without a system, what starts as provision can lead to pressure and loss. Joseph's system sustained the impact of his gift long after the moment of favor passed.

If you want to grow, don't just rely on moments of inspiration; build repeatable structures. Turn your gift into a framework. Design what you do so others can do it too. Systems don't restrict your calling; instead, they multiply it.

Biblical Systems That Sustained Impact

Throughout Scripture, we see how both God and godly leaders implemented systems to preserve blessings, sustain growth, and support expansion:

- Creation Order (Genesis 1). From the very beginning, God demonstrated that He works through process, order, and systems. The divine rhythm of work and rest established by creation serves as the framework for understanding how time and productivity function. As one preacher insightfully said, *"God doesn't govern the world by miracles, but by principles and processes."* Indeed, we live in the solar system, not the "solar miracle." Everything from the orbit of planets to the rising of the sun operates on predictable, measurable laws. That's why we can launch a satellite to Jupiter and calculate its arrival down to the second—because systems bring consistency, order, and predictability. Psalm 148:6 declares, *"He established them for ever and ever. He gave them laws they will always have to obey."* The entire universe is a testament to God's system: stable, structured, and sustained. And if God works through systems, we are wise to build our lives, businesses, and ministries on intentional design, not wishful thinking.

- Delegation under Moses (Exodus 18:13–27). When the responsibility of judging the people became overwhelming, Jethro advised Moses to delegate authority by appointing capable leaders over thousands, hundreds, fifties, and tens. This decentralized structure created a system of tiered leadership that made justice accessible and sustainable. It prevented burnout, empowered others, and ensured that the people's needs were met efficiently. This model allowed Moses to focus on higher-level issues while trained leaders handled routine matters, preserving both Moses and the mission.

- David's Governmental System (1 Chronicles 23–27). David implemented a robust national framework by dividing responsibilities among various leaders and officials. He appointed commanders over thousands for the army, gatekeepers for the city, overseers for public works, treasurers for the temple and royal storehouses, and record keepers for civil affairs. David was a seasoned warrior who had fought under Saul's kingship and famously conquered Goliath. He understood that one warrior could defeat a thousand, but two together could defeat ten thousand (Deuteronomy 32:30). This revealed to him a profound principle: without structure and shared leadership, even the most anointed vision would collapse under its own weight. Each role in his government had defined duties and levels of authority, creating a layered leadership system. This organizational clarity enabled the nation to function smoothly, scale its operations, and maintain justice and order, whether in times of peace or in preparation for future building projects like the temple.

- Worship and Priesthood System (1 Chronicles 25:1–8) — David's worship system was deeply structured. David was a passionate worshiper who knew how to touch God's heart through his gift. However, he also understood that his personal passion alone could not reach or transform the entire nation. One man's worship can inspire, but it takes a structured system to shape a nation. He appointed 24 divisions of priests and Levite musicians to serve in rotating shifts, ensuring that worship before the Lord continued day and night without interruption. These divisions were carefully organized through casting lots, reflecting fairness and divine order. Additionally, training was provided so that each group upheld the same standards of excellence. This system not only prevented burnout but also created a spiritual rhythm and continuity in Israel's relationship with God.

McDonald's is not just a fast-food chain; it's a global system built on precision, duplication, and consistency. Every McDonald's restaurant, whether in New York or Nairobi, operates on the same principles: standardized menus, identical kitchen layouts, uniform employee training, and strict quality control. This allows the company to offer the same customer experience worldwide, regardless of location or manager. What makes McDonald's incredibly powerful is that its real business isn't food, it's systems. The founder didn't just sell burgers; he sold a repeatable, proven model that anyone could implement. Because of this, McDonald's has expanded into over 100 countries with more than 38,000 locations, generating billions in revenue. Their success is proof that when you systematize a gift or product, you don't just grow, you scale with *predictable excellence.*

Amazon's dominance in global commerce is driven by its world-class Fulfillment System—a logistical masterpiece that enables millions of products to be delivered in 1–2 days. Behind every "Buy Now" button is a web of automated warehouses, inventory tracking, packaging lines, and delivery algorithms. From the moment you place an order, Amazon's system identifies the nearest warehouse, locates the item, assigns robotic arms to retrieve it, package it, and hands it off to a courier, all with minimal human involvement. This level of speed and accuracy isn't possible without a finely-tuned system. What Amazon built wasn't just an online bookstore; it created an engine of predictable performance, able to handle explosive growth without collapsing under pressure. Amazon proves that wealth isn't just in what you sell but in how efficiently and repeatedly you can deliver it.

What McDonald's and Amazon have in common is predictability. Both companies took something simple, a burger, a product, and built a repeatable, scalable system around it. That system allowed them to expand globally, maintain excellence, and multiply income without depending on a single person's daily effort. Now imagine applying that same principle to your gift—whether it's writing, teaching, coaching, or ministering. Your gift is powerful, but without a system, it can stay limited to one location, one person, or one moment.

When you build a system around your gift, whether it's through a book funnel, coaching program, online course, or speaking framework, you move from *serving people one by one* to *impacting* hundreds or thousands consistently. Just like McDonald's doesn't need the founder to make every burger, and Amazon doesn't need Jeff Bezos to ship every package, you don't need to be present for your gift to produce fruit. Systems allow you to duplicate your message, multiply your reach, and ultimately generate income and influence without burnout. The same God who designed the universe with systems invites you to steward your gift with the same level of order and intentionality.

Expand Through Investment

Joseph's economic model in Genesis 41 was more than a survival plan; it was a masterclass in strategic investment. During the seven years of abundance, he instituted a national policy to store 20% of all grain, systematically collecting and preserving it in cities across Egypt. At first, this may seem like a simple act of preservation for the years of famine. But a closer look reveals a deeper intention: Joseph wasn't just preparing for a crisis; he was positioning Egypt for dominance. The stored grain became more than food; it became leverage. Rather than treating the surplus as a mere emergency supply, Joseph treated it as a future commodity. This resource would later be sold, traded, and used to expand Egypt's influence, wealth, and political reach. His foresight turned temporary excess into lasting power.

When the famine struck, that stored grain became a source of provision, a source of cash flow, and a source of prosperity.

- Source of Provision: Genesis 41:54–56 reveals that the grain stored during Egypt's years of abundance served a vital purpose—it sustained the nation during the famine. While neighboring lands suffered, Egypt remained stable and secure. Joseph's strategic foresight created a buffer of protection, ensuring that the people had food when it mattered most. His planning preserved lives and upheld the nation's internal peace during a crisis.

- Sources of Cash Flow: The grain reserve wasn't simply distributed—it was sold. As people from surrounding nations came to buy food, Egypt experienced a steady influx of cash flow. What began as storage became a national revenue engine. Joseph's approach turned surplus into a stream of income that strengthened Egypt's economy, allowing the country to thrive financially even in a global crisis.

- Source of prosperity: Beyond provision and profit, Joseph's grain strategy elevated Egypt to a place of regional economic power. The grain became a tradeable commodity that attracted nations and positioned Egypt as a hub of commerce. Wealth increased, influence expanded, and Egypt gained political leverage. Joseph's system laid the foundation for lasting prosperity by turning temporary excess into long-term dominance.

Just as Joseph didn't consume everything during the years of abundance but chose to invest the surplus for the future, you must treat your gift and potential the same way. Many people are gifted, but few are strategic. Joseph's decision to store 20% of the grain during the good years was not random; it was rooted in a principle that mirrors a modern wealth-building rule: saving or investing at least 20% of your income. While others may have wanted to enjoy the abundance, Joseph resisted the urge to spend the surplus on temporary pleasures. Instead of using extra resources to buy what he wanted, he preserved them for what the nation would eventually need. This level of discipline and foresight positioned Egypt to not only survive the famine but thrive in the crisis.

In the same way, your gift, whether it's writing, teaching, speaking, or creating, must be treated like a resource with long-term value. Don't waste your extra time, energy, or finances on things that make you feel good in the moment. Invest them in your growth. That means learning, creating systems, building content, improving your craft, and sowing into others. The grain Joseph stored became a source of influence, income, and access. Likewise, the ideas, skills, and discipline you invest today can become books, businesses, platforms, or a generational legacy tomorrow.

Although ancient Egypt lacked digital tools, Joseph invested in infrastructure, storage systems, and administrative processes, the "technology" of his day. Genesis 41:48-49 says Joseph gathered grain "like the sand of the sea" and stored it in each city, which implies logistics planning, building storage facilities, and managing data through organized recordkeeping. This was an advanced operational system for that time. Joseph didn't just have a good idea—he used the best tools and systems available to bring that idea to life.

Today, that same principle applies to your gift. Suppose you're a writer, speaker, teacher, or entrepreneur. In that case, you must invest in technology that multiplies your reach and effectiveness, whether that's publishing tools, video production software, automation systems, online platforms, or AI tools. Just like Joseph's grain needed proper storage, your gift needs the right platforms and digital structure to scale.

Many people resist new technology due to fear of change, complexity, or failure. But the truth is, technology will continually advance, whether you're ready or not. And those who refuse to adapt will inevitably be left behind. Innovation doesn't wait for permission. It favors the bold, the curious, and the prepared. History is full of examples: Blockbuster was once a household name in video rentals, but its passivity to embrace digital streaming allowed Netflix, a company that leaned into new technology, to take over the market completely. Similarly, Kodak, despite inventing the first digital camera, clung to film photography and lost its relevance when the world shifted. Even individuals are not exempt: talented professionals who refused to learn digital tools, social media, or online platforms have seen their opportunities shrink while others thrive. As Joseph used the best systems of his day to secure the future, you must be willing to embrace new tools to steward your gift in this era. Technology isn't the enemy of your calling—it's a vehicle for your expansion.

Takeaway: When God blesses you with abundance, it is not only for consumption, but also for investment. The way you steward surplus today determines your capacity to influence tomorrow. Strategic saving and wise planning in the present create open doors in the future.

Application Insight:

- What is your "grain" right now?

- What resource or surplus do you currently have that can be preserved or invested?

- Are you creating systems to manage your increase?

- How can you turn your current blessings into sustainable impact?

Chapter Five

Perpetual Revenue

Introduction

After Joseph rose to power, he understood that saving grain alone wouldn't provide enough cash flow to support the population or create lasting wealth. This chapter emphasizes the need to let your talents evolve and generate diverse products. It also explores how the value of your offerings increases in proportion to your personal growth and development.

Perpetual revenue is income that continues even after your effort ends. It is wealth that is produced through systems, stewardship, and strategic thinking; resources that continue to grow and multiply, even when you are not directly working on them. This chapter explores how we can create lasting wealth and build legacies through the same principles that Joseph used in ancient Egypt.

The story of Joseph offers a profound lesson in the power of long-term strategy. Joseph's management of Egypt's grain during the years of abundance wasn't just a temporary measure—it was a masterfully crafted plan that created lasting prosperity. His wisdom transformed what was initially a surplus into a perpetual source of revenue, providing for Egypt and neighboring nations. Joseph's approach wasn't about chasing quick profits; it was about building systems that would generate ongoing wealth over time. His genius lay in creating perpetual revenue.

Joseph's wealth didn't come from an instant windfall. It was the result of careful preparation, strategic management, and the wisdom to turn scarcity into abundance. His story demonstrates that true wealth is not about quick, short-term gains but about creating a foundation for sustained prosperity. His wisdom in stewarding the resources Egypt had and his foresight in preparing for future scarcity laid the groundwork for long-term success—not just for him, but for his entire nation.

The Stairs of Value

Joseph's wisdom lay not just in surviving the famine, but in creating a system that outlived the immediate crisis. His grain became a generational resource that could be traded and used for years.

Let's break down the brilliance of Joseph's strategy further. When he first began storing grain in preparation for the famine, the value of grain was ordinary. It was abundant and stored for future use. But as time went on and famine approached, the value of the grain began to rise exponentially. What was once a common commodity became a rare and highly sought-after resource.

In Genesis 47:16, when the famine hit and money was depleted, Joseph's grain was exchanged for livestock. A year later, it became so valuable that Egyptians traded their land and eventually themselves for it (Genesis 47:19). This shows how scarcity, combined with timing, enhances the value of an asset. Joseph understood the law of scarcity; he knew that resources can gain much more value when they are rare, especially during moments of dire need.

This is where we see the *"Stairs of Value"* principle in full effect. The first stage in value creation is about timing and management. Joseph didn't release all the grain at once; he did so in stages, at the most strategic moments. The second stage is about personal growth and development. As Joseph grew in wisdom and leadership, he became the primary asset who could influence everything else. This dual approach, combined with timing and personal development, formed the foundation of Joseph's perpetual revenue model.

Creating perpetual revenue isn't about instantly monetizing your gifts. It's about building value over time and allowing your products, services, or skills to evolve. Joseph's journey starts with a gift: his ability to interpret dreams. This gift wasn't immediately monetizable, but it was extraordinarily valuable in the proper context. Initially, Joseph's gifts were given freely, without any compensation. But as time went on, Joseph's gift evolved from something intangible, his dream interpretation, into something tangible: "the grain", and later, bread, which is a refined and processed product that provided more nourishment and value. Each stage in Joseph's journey represents a stair of value; his gift evolving into something more structured, more impactful, and more valuable.

The First Stair: Dream interpretation

The first stage begins with offering your gift freely. This is the first step on the Stairs of Value. It's often the hardest stage because it demands faith in the process, especially when you're not receiving monetary compensation right away.

At this stage, your value isn't yet being measured in dollars; it's being measured in trust. You're not just building a product; you're building relationships. Like Joseph interpreting dreams for free in prison, this stage is about proving your worth through action, not just intention.

Though you're giving your value away for free, it must still be exceptional. Why? Because excellence, even in the smallest actions, will draw people to you. Word-of-mouth will become your first form of marketing. The trust you build will lay the foundation for everything that follows.

This stage is often the longest because you're not just building a product, you're building trust. And once trust is established, it becomes the key to unlocking revenue that can sustain and scale. Just like Joseph, who faithfully interpreted dreams in prison without asking for anything in return, you start by showing up, serving with consistency, and demonstrating your value. Over time, your credibility will become undeniable. During this phase, actions like hosting seminars, offering targeted interventions, providing small training sessions, and actively helping your community will help solidify your reputation and build lasting relationships.

Here are some practical steps to take during the first stage of offering your gift freely and building trust, based on the principles in the passage:

1. Show Up Consistently

- Action: Commit to consistently show up and offer your expertise or service, even without immediate monetary gain.

- Example: Set aside regular time to share your knowledge or skills, whether it's through social media posts, blogs, community events, or informal gatherings.

- Benefit: Consistency helps build trust and reliability with your audience.

2. Serve Others Without Expecting Payment

- Action: Like Joseph, offer your gift freely without expecting compensation at first. This could mean offering a free service, volunteering, or providing advice or training to others at no charge.

- Example: Volunteer to speak at local events, mentor someone in your field, or offer free coaching sessions.

- Benefit: Serving others for free helps you establish credibility and strengthens your relationships.

3. Focus on Excellence

- Action: Even though you're giving your value away for free, make sure it's delivered at a high standard. Strive for excellence in every small action, as this will be noticed and appreciated.

- Example: When offering free advice, ensure it's well-researched and tailored to the person's needs. If you're creating content, make it polished, engaging, and helpful.

- Benefit: Excellence attracts attention, builds credibility, and fosters word-of-mouth marketing, which will expand your reach.

4. Build Relationships, Not Just Products

- Action: Take the time to build genuine relationships with people. Focus on understanding their needs, providing value, and being a source of help.

- Example: Engage with people in meaningful conversations, whether it's on social media or in person. Ask about their challenges and offer solutions or advice.

- Benefit: Building relationships forms a loyal community that trusts you, which is the foundation for long-term success.

5. Use Word-of-Mouth as Your First Marketing Tool

- Action: As you serve with excellence, encourage satisfied individuals to share their experience with others. Create an environment where word-of-mouth recommendations are a natural result of your value.

- Example: After a free session or service, ask your clients or audience for testimonials or referrals.

- Benefit: Word-of-mouth marketing is one of the most potent forms of promotion, as it's built on trust and genuine recommendations.

6. Offer Seminars, Training, and Interventions

- Action: Host seminars or workshops, or offer small training sessions and targeted interventions for individuals or groups, even at no cost initially.

- Example: Offer free community seminars or webinars in your area of expertise, where people can learn and interact with you directly.

- Benefit: These activities not only demonstrate your value but also provide an opportunity to build relationships and gain credibility within your community.

7. Engage in Community Involvement

- Action: Actively participate in community events or local initiatives that align with your skill set or gift. Give freely of your time and expertise to help others in your community.

- Example: Volunteer at local nonprofits or collaborate with local businesses to host events that serve the public.

- Benefit: Community involvement builds your reputation as a genuine contributor and trusted leader, and opens doors for future opportunities.

8. Develop Your Personal Brand Through Storytelling

- Action: Share your personal journey, the struggles, and successes that led you to where you are today. Storytelling humanizes your brand and builds deeper connections with others.

- Example: Share your experiences and lessons learned through blogs, podcasts, or social media posts to let others see and understand your passion and expertise.

- Benefit: Personal stories foster emotional connections, allowing people to see you not just as a service provider but as someone they can trust and relate to.

9. Be Patient and Trust the Process

- Action: Recognize that the journey of building trust is often slow and requires patience. Remain committed to offering value without focusing solely on immediate returns.

- Example: Stay consistent with your efforts, even if you don't see immediate financial rewards. Trust that your reputation will grow over time.

- Benefit: Patience allows you to build deep trust and a solid foundation for scaling your efforts in the future

The Second Stair: From Dream to Grain

As time progresses, you'll begin to develop and release a second product or set of products, whether tangible or intangible, that carries even greater value. This new product is enriched by the lessons you've learned, the experiences you've gained, and the credibility you've built through your initial work. By now, your audience or clientele knows your character, trusts your insights, and is ready to invest in what you have to offer. This is your "grain", your refined, market-ready product. Unlike your first contributions, which were freely given, this one is ripe for monetization. Your unwavering integrity, well-placed advice, and commitment to serving others with love have paved the way for long-term success and meaningful, lasting impact.

Here are practical steps to help you develop and release your second product ("grain"), based on the principles in the passage:

1. Reflect on Your Journey and Gather Insights

- Action: Take time to reflect on what you've learned through your first product or service. What feedback have you received from your audience? What lessons have you learned about your process, your target audience, and what works well?

- Example: Review customer testimonials, conduct surveys, or analyze data from your first offering to understand what resonated most with your audience.

- Benefit: This will help you refine your approach and create a product that is better suited to meet the needs of your audience.

2. Identify Your Refined, Market-Ready Product

- Action: Now that you have experience and insight, identify your next product or service that can be improved and enhanced. It should be something more refined, built on the foundation of your first offering, but with added value that addresses a broader or deeper need.

- Example: If your first offering was a free introductory workshop on fashion design, your next step could be a premium, in-depth course or a consulting service for those who want more personalized guidance.

- Benefit: This refined product will be more attractive to people who are already familiar with your work and ready to invest in a more specialized offering.

3. Ensure Your Product Reflects Your Growth and Expertise

- Action: Make sure that your second product reflects your personal growth, the lessons you've learned, and your increased credibility. It should be a product that shows your development, not just a continuation of what you've already done.

- Example: Create a new, high-quality digital product such as an online course or workshop series that highlights your evolution as a leader or expert in your field. This could incorporate new techniques, advanced tips, or insights you've gained.

- Benefit: This product will be perceived as more valuable, demonstrating that you've gained more experience and have a deeper understanding of your subject.

4. Strengthen Relationships with Your Audience

- Action: Deepen your relationship with your audience by engaging with them in more personalized and meaningful ways. They need to know that they can trust you and that your second product will meet their needs.

- Example: Regularly engage with your audience through email newsletters, live Q&A sessions, or personalized communication on social media. Share updates, give sneak peeks of your new product, and ask for feedback.

- Benefit: By continuing to build trust and rapport, you ensure that when your second product is ready, your audience will be eager to buy because they feel connected to you.

5. Create a Pricing Strategy That Reflects the Value

- Action: Develop a pricing strategy for your second product that aligns with its increased value and reflects the quality and impact it will have on your audience. The price should be fair, acknowledging the time, expertise, and growth you've invested.

- Example: If your first offering was free or low-cost, your second product can be priced higher to reflect its added value. For instance, if your initial service was a free consultation, the second could be a paid, in-depth strategy session or a premium membership for ongoing coaching.

- Benefit: Pricing your second product correctly allows you to both honor your time and expertise while also ensuring it is positioned as a premium offering.

6. Market the Product with Focused Messaging

- Action: Craft your marketing message around the value and impact your second product will bring. Highlight how it's more refined and strategically designed to provide better results for your audience.

- Example: Use your previous experiences and successes to showcase testimonials or case studies from those who benefited from your initial work. Show how your second product will take them to the next level.

- Benefit: Well-crafted marketing and messaging will make your audience feel like your new product is exactly what they need, and they'll be ready to invest.

7. Deliver Your Product with Excellence

- Action: Ensure that the delivery of your second product meets the highest standards of quality. This is where your integrity and commitment to excellence shine through. Whether it's a service, digital product, or physical product, the experience should be seamless and impactful.

- Example: If your product is an online course, ensure it's well-organized, engaging, and professionally produced. If it's a service, ensure your processes are streamlined, and the results are evident.

- Benefit: By delivering on your promises and providing excellent value, you reinforce your reputation as a trusted expert, making it more likely that customers will return or recommend your product.

8. Use Social Proof and Testimonials to Build Trust

- Action: Use testimonials, reviews, and case studies to demonstrate how your product has already impacted others. Social proof helps reduce skepticism and builds trust for potential buyers.

- Example: If you've already served a few clients or users of your product, ask them for testimonials or feedback that you can share in your marketing materials.

- Benefit: Social proof can be one of the most powerful tools to boost conversions and reassure potential customers that they are making a worthwhile investment.

9. Reinvest in Your Growth and Development

- Action: Reinvest the revenue you generate from your second product into your own growth. This will allow you to continually evolve and improve your offerings.

- Example: Use your profits to attend workshops, hire mentors, or invest in tools that will help you refine your products or expand your reach.

- Benefit: As you continue to grow, your future products will continue to increase in value, helping you build a sustainable business that scales over time.

In Summary:

To develop and release your "grain," focus on creating a product that reflects your growth and credibility. Offer value through strong relationships, refined products, and consistent excellence. With a strategic approach to pricing, marketing, and delivery, you can successfully move to the next stair of your business journey, leading to sustainable, long-term success.

The Third Stair: From Grain to Bread

The next stair is to transform your grain into bread, turning your refined raw material into a high impact, finished product. Bread is no longer just a provision; it is nourishment shaped with care, insight, and excellence. At this stage, what you offer is not only useful but transformational. It bears the imprint of maturity, depth, and credibility. This could take the form of a premium course, an immersive workshop, a best-selling book, or any product that combines mastery with experience. What sets this stage apart is that it confirms your authority, multiplies your reach, and becomes the foundation for a long-term, recurring income stream. Just as Joseph released grain strategically during the famine, you now release your "bread" at peak value and demand, cementing your place as a provider of lasting solutions.

Here are some practical steps to help you transform your "grain" into "bread" turning your refined product into a high-impact, finished product that creates lasting value:

1. Refine Your Offering to Meet a Deep Need

- Action: Ensure that your product (now your "bread") addresses a transformational need for your audience. This is no longer just a solution; it should offer a lasting change or improvement in your clients' lives.

- Example: If you've been offering free advice or introductory services, your next step might be to create a premium course or a consultation package that dives deeper into specific problems your audience faces. You should craft your product so that it provides not just information but actionable steps for profound change.

- Benefit: This ensures that your offering has real value that makes a lasting difference, not just a temporary fix.

2. Ensure Excellence and Mastery in Delivery

- Action: Take the time to perfect your product. This is your opportunity to showcase your expertise and craft something that reflects your growth and experience.

- Example: If you're launching a course, make sure the content is well-researched, structured, and presented in a way that's engaging. If it's a book, ensure it's well-edited, with a clear, professional layout and packaging. Put extra care into every detail, as excellence at this stage will help you stand out.

- Benefit: By delivering a high-quality product, you establish credibility and trust, which are key to scaling your business.

3. Position Yourself as an Authority

- Action: Use your experience and expertise to position yourself as a thought leader in your field. Your "bread" should carry the weight of your authority, reflecting the maturity you've gained through your journey.

- Example: Public speaking, guest appearances on podcasts, or writing guest articles for reputable platforms can help build your profile. Share case studies, testimonials, and real-life examples to showcase how your product has transformed others.

- Benefit: As you build your authority, people will start seeing you as the go-to expert, which will help you reach a wider audience and establish yourself as a leader in your niche.

4. Release at Peak Demand

- Action: Just as Joseph released his grain strategically during a time of famine, ensure that you release your "bread" at the right time to maximize demand. This could be after building anticipation, creating a waiting list, or launching a pre-order campaign.

- Example: Plan a launch event—whether virtual or in person—where you unveil your product, emphasizing its unique value and timing. Use your platform to drum up excitement and build anticipation in advance.

- Benefit: By releasing your product at peak demand, you position yourself to achieve maximum sales and impact, while cementing your reputation as a provider of valuable solutions.

5. Create a Scalable Income Stream

- Action: Ensure that your product has the potential for recurring revenue or scalability. This can take the form of subscription models, ongoing services, or affiliate programs.

- Example: If your product is an online course, consider creating a membership site where subscribers pay for continuous access to new content. If it's a workshop, offer advanced follow-up sessions or ongoing coaching for a fee.

- Benefit: Scalable income streams ensure that your business doesn't rely on a single transaction, but generates consistent, recurring revenue over time.

6. Use Testimonials and Social Proof

- Action: As you release your bread (premium product), leverage testimonials, success stories, and social proof to demonstrate the value of what you've created.

- Example: Encourage customers to share their results, or ask satisfied clients for video testimonials. Feature these prominently on your website, social media, and sales pages.

- Benefit: Social proof builds trust with potential buyers and shows them that your product delivers on its promises.

7. Develop an Effective Marketing Strategy

- Action: Craft a strong marketing strategy that highlights the unique value and transformation your product offers. Focus on the impact your product will have on the lives of your customers.

- Example: Build an email campaign or create a series of content-driven posts that speak to the needs of your audience and how your product can meet those needs. Use testimonials, sneak peeks, and content that showcases your product's actual value.

- Benefit: Effective marketing will help position your product as a must-have solution, attracting more people to invest in it.

8. Focus on Long-Term Customer Relationships

- Action: Once you release your "bread," it's essential to focus on building long-term relationships with your customers. Treat them not just as one-time buyers, but as partners in your journey.

- Example: After someone purchases your product, offer them follow-up support, feedback surveys, or exclusive offers for future products. Stay engaged with them through regular communication, delivering value that helps them continue to benefit from your offering.

- Benefit: By creating loyal customers, you build a community that will continue to support you and purchase future products or services.

9. Analyze and Iterate for Improvement

- Action: After releasing your product, take the time to analyze its performance and gather feedback for improvement. Even the best products can be refined over time.

- Example: Use analytics tools to track customer engagement, sales, and feedback. Adjust your product or marketing strategies based on customer responses and evolving needs.

- Benefit: Continuous improvement ensures that your product remains relevant and valuable, increasing its lifetime value and your ability to generate income from it.

In Summary:

To transform your grain into bread, focus on creating a high-impact, transformational product that reflects your growth, mastery, and authority. Release it at the right time, with a solid marketing strategy, and ensure it has the potential for scalable, recurring revenue. As you establish yourself as an authority and continue to build relationships, your product will not only succeed in the short term but also achieve long-term success. Still, it will also lay the foundation for long-term, sustainable growth.

The fourth and on stairs: "The Cake"

Once you have established credibility and released your transformational "bread," the next step often comes naturally. The value of your offering is so undeniable, so impactful, that people will start reaching out to you for more. Your bread has proven itself to be exceptional, and now clients and potential clients are coming to you, not only for the original product but for new variations of it— products of increasing value. Your creative potential becomes the wellspring of opportunities.

As your bread rises in value, you will find that your clients are no longer just waiting for you to create; they are guiding the way. Their needs and requests will start to shape the next phase of your journey. They will tell you what they want, which feeds your creativity and pushes your boundaries further. For example, a company might reach out to request a specialized course tailored to a specific group of employees, or a group of talented professionals may want you to supervise and mentor their work. These requests act as stepping stones, propelling you to new heights.

What makes this stage so exciting is that the sky becomes the limit. With each new challenge, each new request, your creativity and experience continue to expand. Your clients are now not only the recipients of your value, but they are the catalysts for your growth. Their input refines and enhances what you offer, and in turn, you develop even greater products that meet their evolving needs. As you continue to innovate and elevate your offerings, the staircase of value keeps ascending. Your path is now guided by the very people you serve, and their needs continue to push you higher on the stairs of success, opening doors to even more lucrative opportunities.

Here are practical steps to help you progress from the "bread" stage to the "Cake" stage, where the value of your offerings is undeniable, and your clients' needs and requests shape opportunities:

1. Leverage the Success of Your Previous Products

- Action: Recognize the impact your "bread" has had. If it's successful, it means you've built a solid foundation of trust and credibility. Start by gathering insights from your existing customers—listen to what they have to say.

Understand how your product has helped them, and more importantly, what gaps still need to be filled.

- Example: Send surveys, ask for testimonials, or reach out for honest feedback on what your product could improve or how it could better serve their needs.

- Benefit: Knowing precisely what your customers are asking for helps you understand the evolutionary path of your next offering. It ensures your product remains relevant and meets a real demand.

2. Open the Door for Customization

- Action: As your credibility grows, start offering customization options for your product or service. Clients might want a version tailored to their specific needs. This not only adds value but deepens your relationship with your clients.

- Example: Develop packages where clients can request tailored services—like personalized coaching, industry-specific workshops, or exclusive training sessions.

- Benefit: Customization not only adds higher value but also positions your business as an adaptive, client-centered brand, making your offerings more appealing and long-lasting.

3. Foster Strong Client Relationships

- Action: At this stage, your clients aren't just waiting for you to create—they're actively guiding the direction of your business. Engage regularly with them to understand their evolving needs and shape your next steps accordingly.

- Example: Schedule check-ins, host focus groups, or set up casual conversations with top clients. Dive into what challenges they are facing now and how your offerings can evolve to meet those needs.

- Benefit: Clients who feel heard and valued are more likely to become repeat customers and even brand ambassadors. These deep relationships foster loyalty and amplify your impact.

4. Expand Your Offerings Based on Client Requests

- Action: Use your clients' requests and feedback to create new variations of your product or service. Your creativity should be fueled by their needs, pushing you to improve and innovate continuously.

- Example: If your clients are asking for more advanced topics, consider creating specialized workshops, VIP consulting packages, or a membership program that provides continuous support.

- Benefit: These new offerings not only serve your clients better but also signal your commitment to growth. They enhance your brand's value by demonstrating your continuous evolution to meet customer needs.

5. Innovate and Elevate Your Brand

- Action: Keep pushing the boundaries of what you offer. As you progress, your brand should evolve to reflect your new creative heights. Innovation is essential to stay relevant, keep your customers engaged, and expand your reach.

- Example: Introduce new features like interactive learning tools, group coaching sessions, or online platforms that make your offerings more immersive and dynamic.

- Benefit: Continuous innovation keeps your brand fresh, while also attracting new customers and ensuring your existing ones stay loyal and engaged.

6. Empower Your Clients to Be Your Ambassadors

- Action: Let your satisfied clients become your most powerful advocates. Use their success stories as testimonials to show how your products have transformed their lives or businesses.

- Example: Offer referral bonuses, exclusive content, or discounts to clients who help spread the word about your offerings.

- Benefit: Word-of-mouth marketing from satisfied customers is priceless. It organically expands your audience, building trust and credibility for your brand.

7. Create Long-Term Programs and Partnerships

- Action: Build long-term programs or partnerships that generate revenue without requiring constant involvement. Consider models like subscriptions, affiliate partnerships, or repeat-service agreements.

- Example: If you offer a course, launch a subscription model for monthly access to new content and updates. Alternatively, create affiliate programs where other influencers or educators promote your products in exchange for a commission.

- Benefit: Long-term programs ensure recurring income, allowing you to plan and invest in future growth, while partnerships expand your reach and credibility.

8. Tap Into New Markets or Industries

- Action: Use the foundation and credibility you've built to explore new markets and industries. Your product's success gives you the confidence to branch out into new areas, expanding your influence and customer base.

- Example: If you've been offering a personal coaching program, consider adapting it for corporate training, or if your course is focused on one niche, explore creating a similar course for an entirely different, yet related, field.

- Benefit: Expanding into new markets opens up new revenue streams and gives your brand flexibility and versatility, positioning you as a leader in multiple sectors.

9. Focus on Recurring Revenue

- Action: Shift your focus to creating recurring revenue streams—products or services that generate consistent income, such as subscriptions, membership sites, or ongoing services.

- Example: Launch a monthly membership where clients access exclusive resources, webinars, or continuous support. This ensures ongoing engagement and secures a predictable revenue stream.

- Benefit: Recurring revenue offers financial stability, helping you forecast income and make strategic investments in your business's future growth.

In Summary:

As your business evolves and clients start to actively guide your growth, use their feedback and requests to innovate and improve your offerings continuously. Empower your clients to become your biggest advocates, expand into new markets, and create recurring revenue models to ensure long-term success. By pushing the boundaries of creativity, building lasting relationships, and focusing on continuous improvement, you'll not only grow your business but cement your position as a trusted provider in your field.

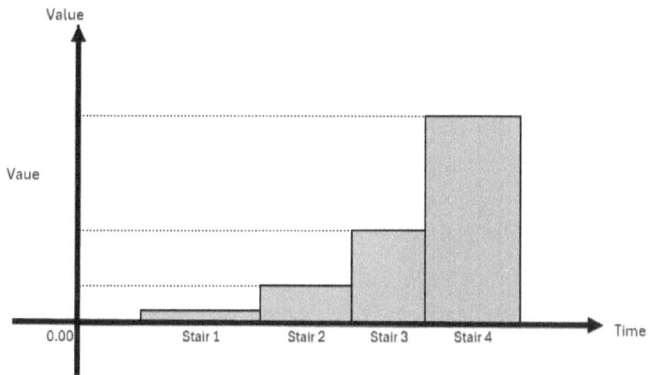

Personal Growth as the Foundation of Value

Joseph's personal growth was essential to his success. His ability to manage resources, make tough decisions, and lead an entire nation all stemmed from his character and wisdom, both of which were shaped by the challenges he faced. Remember, he was betrayed by his brothers, falsely accused by Potiphar's wife, and forgotten by the cupbearer. Each trial tested his integrity, but rather than allowing bitterness to take root, Joseph let his character grow stronger. It was through these personal trials that Joseph learned how to manage people, lead with wisdom, and act with integrity.

Your personal character growth is directly tied to the value of the products you create. As you grow in wisdom, discipline, and leadership, your ability to manage resources, make informed decisions, and leave a lasting impact also strengthens. The more solid your foundation in these areas, the more effectively you can craft offerings that resonate deeply with others and create a meaningful, enduring impact. And with that growth, your price tag naturally increases. The products you make are no longer just functional; they become premium offerings, imbued with the wisdom of experience, the integrity of your leadership, and the depth of your personal development.

The more you evolve, the more your offerings are seen as irreplaceable and highly valuable. Each product you create carries not only your expertise but your growth journey. As you rise in stature, so does the value of everything you offer. Whether it's a service, a course, or a product, the price reflects not just the effort but the transformation you've undergone, making it worth every investment.

Joseph's story teaches us that the external wealth we accumulate is a reflection of the internal growth we undergo. To produce lasting value, we must be willing to grow, learn, and develop.

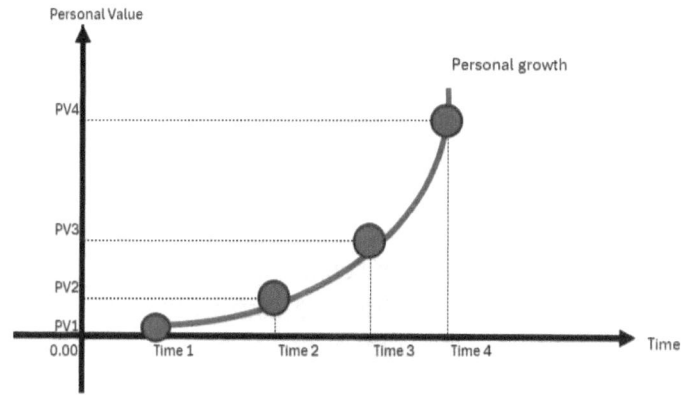

Practical Steps for Personal Growth as the Foundation of Value

Joseph's personal growth played a pivotal role in his success. Through betrayal, false accusations, and being forgotten, he learned how to manage resources, make tough decisions, and lead a nation. His challenges didn't break him; they refined him, shaping his wisdom, integrity, and leadership abilities. This kind of growth is what ultimately fueled his ability to create lasting prosperity. Your own personal development will directly influence the value of the products and services you create, and here's how you can leverage that growth.

1. View Challenges as Opportunities for Transformation

173

- Action: When you face obstacles or setbacks, don't resist them—use them as opportunities for personal and professional growth. Each challenge is a chance to strengthen your character and leadership.

- Example: After a failed product launch or a negative review, take time to reflect on what you can learn from the experience. How can this help you adapt and improve?

- Benefit: Just like Joseph's trials shaped his wisdom, embracing challenges will help you grow in resilience and resourcefulness, which ultimately strengthens your offerings.

2. Commit to Lifelong Learning

- Action: Develop a habit of learning and evolving. Whether it's through books, courses, mentorship, or simply reflecting on your experiences, continual education sharpens your skills and broadens your perspective.

- Example: Dedicate 30 minutes a day to reading or taking an online course related to your field. Surround yourself with people who challenge you to grow.

- Benefit: The more knowledge and expertise you gain, the more valuable your products and services become, allowing you to offer more sophisticated and impactful solutions.

3. Strengthen Your Emotional Intelligence

- Action: Focus on improving your emotional intelligence (EQ). The more in tune you are with your own emotions and those of others, the better equipped you'll be to manage relationships, make decisions, and navigate challenges.

- Example: Practice active listening and empathy in your interactions. When faced with conflict or feedback, respond thoughtfully and calmly, considering both logical and emotional aspects.

- Benefit: A high EQ will make you a better leader, help you build stronger relationships, and ensure that your products not only meet needs but resonate deeply with your audience.

4. Lead with Integrity and Authenticity

- Action: Let integrity be the cornerstone of your leadership. Lead by example and ensure that your decisions reflect your values. Your actions should always align with your vision and beliefs.

- Example: If you're running a business, choose ethical suppliers, deliver on promises, and be transparent in your dealings.

- Benefit: Integrity builds trust, which is essential for long-term success. As your reputation grows, so does the value of your offerings.

5. Build Discipline and Consistency

- Action: Develop the discipline to pursue your goals consistently. Whether it's creating a product, building a brand, or improving a skill, consistency is key to turning small actions into significant results.

- Example: Set daily or weekly goals that help you make steady progress. Whether it's crafting content, engaging with your audience, or refining your product, commit to showing up and delivering consistently.

- Benefit: The more consistently you put in the work, the more refined and valuable your product becomes, ensuring that your efforts compound into long-term success.

6. Reflect and Recognize Your Growth

- Action: Regularly pause to assess how far you've come. Reflect on your personal and professional journey, acknowledging the lessons learned and the growth achieved.

- Example: Keep a growth journal where you track milestones, setbacks, and key moments of learning. Reflect on how these experiences have shaped you and your approach to business.

- Benefit: This reflection will not only boost your confidence but also help you see the deeper value you bring to your products and services. As you grow, your offerings naturally become more unique and irreplaceable.

7. Seek Feedback and Mentorship

- Action: Surround yourself with mentors and trusted advisors who can offer guidance and constructive feedback. A mentor's perspective can accelerate your growth by pointing out blind spots and encouraging you to go further.

- Example: Regularly check in with a mentor or coach who can help you identify areas for improvement and hold you accountable for your goals.

- Benefit: Mentorship provides insight and clarity, helping you navigate challenges with greater wisdom. This guidance also ensures your products are aligned with both your vision and your audience's needs.

8. Align Your Personal and Business Growth

- Action: Ensure that your personal development is aligned with the evolution of your business. As you grow, your company should reflect that growth in both its offerings and its mission.

- Example: If you're growing in emotional intelligence, incorporate that into how you manage your team or communicate with customers. If you're learning new strategies, apply them to improve your product development.

- Benefit: By aligning your inner growth with your business evolution, you create products that are not only high in value but also deeply connected to your authentic vision.

9. Stay Committed to Long-Term Impact

- Action: Shift your focus from short-term gains to creating lasting impact. Consider the legacy you want to build and focus on creating products that will continue to benefit others over time.

- Example: Create evergreen content or long-term coaching programs that will provide sustained value for years to come.

- Benefit: Products that create lasting impact are seen as premium offerings, which significantly raise your value in the market.

In Summary:

Your personal growth is the foundation on which you build lasting value in your products and services. By embracing challenges, committing to continuous learning, and leading with integrity, you enhance your ability to create solutions that not only serve but transform. As you evolve, so too does the value of your offerings. The more you grow, the more irreplaceable your products become, ensuring long-term success and a lasting legacy.

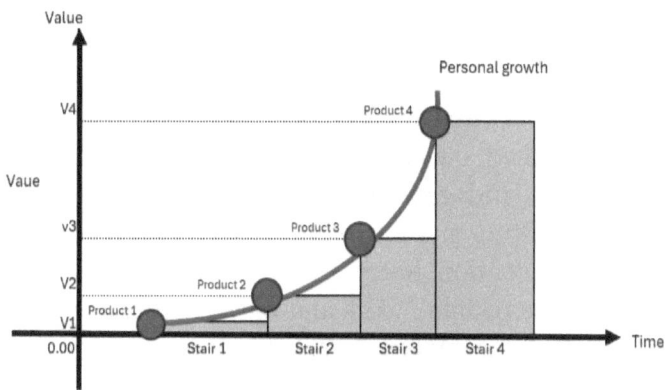

Revenue Sharing Model for perpetual growth

Joseph's system in Genesis 47 is a brilliant example of creating perpetual revenue—a sustainable model that continued to generate wealth for Egypt even long after Joseph's time. When the famine reached its peak, the people of Egypt had spent all their money buying grain from Joseph. Instead of simply continuing to sell grain until it ran out, Joseph designed a revenue-sharing system that would not only sustain the economy through the crisis but also provide long-term financial stability for the nation.

In Genesis 47:24, Joseph established a system where the people worked the land in exchange for 80% of the harvest, with 20% going to Pharaoh. This wasn't just a temporary fix for a dire situation—it was a sustainable system that created ongoing wealth. The 20% that Pharaoh received became a steady, recurring source of income for the state, ensuring Egypt's prosperity even beyond the famine.

This system created a perpetual revenue stream. Once it was established, the people were empowered to continue working the land, generating wealth year after year. The cycle of planting and harvesting didn't rely on Joseph's direct intervention every season—it ran on its own, fueled by the people's work and the structure Joseph set up. This is what makes Joseph's model so powerful: it wasn't just about a one-time sale; it was about creating systems that continue to produce wealth and provide opportunity for future generations. Even after Joseph, Egypt's economy continued to thrive because of the framework he put in place.

Most importantly, Joseph's system wasn't oppressive. It wasn't about Pharaoh taking everything from the people. Instead, it was a shared responsibility: the people worked the land and kept the majority of the harvest, while Pharaoh's share funded the state. They were not just dependent on the state for survival; they were empowered to work, produce, and thrive. They had a stake in the land and the system that allowed them to grow and succeed.

This model teaches us that wealth isn't just about what you own—it's about how you share it. Joseph's system demonstrates that empowering others to succeed alongside you can lead to lasting, shared prosperity. Instead of creating a system that left people dependent on handouts, Joseph created one that allowed everyone to contribute, benefit, and build wealth together.

Joseph's system became the foundation of Egypt's continued success because it was based on partnership and empowerment. People weren't just working for Pharaoh—they were working for themselves, for their families, and for the long-term prosperity of their nation. This mutual benefit made the system sustainable, and it kept producing revenue long after Joseph's direct involvement. This is the essence of perpetual revenue: creating a structure that not only sustains wealth but also empowers others to build alongside you.

Design a Revenue Sharing System

- Action: Create a revenue-sharing structure where both you and your collaborators, employees, or clients benefit from the wealth you generate. This can take many forms, but the core idea is to set up an ongoing, shared model that ensures everyone has a stake in the success of the business.

- Example: If you run a service-based business or a product-driven company, establish a system where your employees, partners, or even customers share in a percentage of profits, not just one-time paychecks or transactions.

- Benefit: By empowering others to benefit from the success of the business, you align everyone's interests, increase motivation, and create a sustainable, growing revenue stream.

2. Offer a Multi-Level Compensation Model

- Action: Implement a multi-level compensation model that rewards people not only for their direct contributions but also for the success of those they help bring on board. This is similar to how Joseph's system allowed for multiple layers of benefits from his initial structure.

- Example: If you're running a network marketing business, for instance, you could create tiers where salespeople earn not only from their own sales but also from the sales made by others they bring into the system. This creates a multi-level income model.

- Benefit: This incentivizes people to bring others into the business, thus creating a network of contributors who all benefit as the company grows. It creates compounding income opportunities and incentivizes teamwork and growth.

3. Empower Your Partners and Employees

- Action: Just as Joseph didn't create dependency, you should design your revenue-sharing model to empower your partners and employees. They should feel like stakeholders in the company, not just people working for you.

- Example: Offer equity or profit-sharing options for key employees or partners. This way, they aren't just earning a salary—they're investing in the company's future, just as the people in Joseph's model invested in Egypt's future by working the land.

- Benefit: Empowering others to share in the profits of the business increases their loyalty and commitment, making them more inclined to help grow the business sustainably.

4. Use Strategic Release of Value

- Action: Similar to how Joseph strategically released grain when it was most needed, you should look for opportune moments to release new products, services, or features to maximize value.

- Example: In your business, plan the release of premium products or exclusive offers based on customer demand or market readiness. Create a sense of scarcity or timing that drives demand and maximizes the impact of each release.

- Benefit: This creates a steady flow of value while ensuring that your offerings are always in demand. Just as Joseph's grain was valuable during the famine, your strategic product releases will keep your business in constant growth mode.

5. Build Systems for Ongoing Wealth Generation

- Action: Develop systems that allow your revenue-sharing model to function independently of your direct involvement. This way, you're not constantly working to generate income—your systems and structure work for you.

- Example: Set up automated processes, such as subscription models, affiliate programs, or licensing agreements, where partners and employees continue to generate wealth without requiring your active involvement.

- Benefit: Like Joseph's grain system, which continued to produce wealth after he set it up, your business model can continue to create wealth year after year with little ongoing intervention from you.

6. Build a Sustainable Partnership Framework

- Action: Create a sustainable partnership framework where everyone involved, from employees to collaborators, has clear roles and benefits. Establish long-term agreements that ensure everyone shares in the rewards of success.

- Example: Create a partnership agreement where collaborators or affiliates earn a percentage of sales, not just for their direct work but for the success of the team they help build. Consider offering tiered rewards based on how much they contribute to the company's growth.

- Benefit: This creates a mutual benefit system where the success of your business depends on everyone's participation. It incentivizes collaboration and encourages everyone to contribute their best work.

7. Reinforce Accountability and Results

- Action: Set up metrics and goals to ensure that all stakeholders are held accountable. This is important in ensuring that the revenue-sharing model stays effective and everyone continues to benefit from their contributions.

- Example: Regularly track sales performance, customer satisfaction, and business growth. Offer bonuses or additional rewards for those who help reach new milestones, such as expanding into new markets or hitting a revenue target.

- Benefit: Accountability ensures that everyone is motivated to keep pushing forward, while reinforcing the long-term nature of the shared prosperity model.

8. Expand the Model to Other Markets or Industries

- Action: As your revenue-sharing system proves successful, consider expanding it into other areas or industries. Just like Joseph's model expanded beyond the immediate famine, you can extend your model to different markets.

- Example: If your business is currently selling products, consider licensing or franchising the revenue-sharing model to other companies, creating a network of businesses all benefiting from your system.

- Benefit: This creates exponential growth by scaling your revenue model across multiple industries, maximizing its reach, and generating multiple streams of income.

9. Focus on Long-Term Sustainability

- Action: Joseph's system wasn't just about solving an immediate crisis; it was about ensuring long-term financial stability. You should focus on building a system that thrives for the long haul.

- Example: Set up investment opportunities, like reinvestment programs for employees, that ensure continuous growth and sustainability. Consider establishing reserve funds or emergency savings for future development or unforeseen challenges.

- Benefit: Long-term thinking ensures that your business remains stable, even in tough times.

This builds a legacy of financial freedom for both you and those involved in your system.

In Summary:

Joseph's revenue-sharing system is a blueprint for creating perpetual revenue that empowers others to succeed while ensuring long-term growth and stability. By incorporating multi-level compensation, customized offerings, and strategic empowerment, you can build a business model that not only creates wealth but sustains it for generations. This approach enables you to provide lasting value, creating a cycle of growth and opportunity for both you and your partners.

In Summary:

In Chapter 5, Perpetual Revenue, we explore how Joseph's story in Genesis 47 exemplifies the power of creating wealth that extends beyond immediate efforts. Joseph's strategy was not just about solving an immediate crisis but about building a long-term system that generated sustainable revenue. His wisdom in managing Egypt's grain and his ability to recognize the value of timing, scarcity, and stewardship allowed him to create a perpetual revenue stream that continued to benefit Egypt and the surrounding nations long after the famine ended.

Joseph's model teaches us the importance of creating systems that work for us over time. The "Stairs of Value" show how value grows incrementally: from offering your gift freely, to creating a refined, market-ready product, to eventually transforming that product into a highly impactful offering. As Joseph did, we must grow in wisdom and character to build lasting, scalable success.

One key principle of this system is shared responsibility, exemplified by Joseph's 80/20 model. He didn't just sell grain during the famine; he empowered the people by creating a revenue-sharing system that allowed them to work the land and prosper, while also ensuring a steady income for the state. This model of partnership, rather than dependence, is crucial to creating perpetual revenue in any business or endeavor.

Joseph's story emphasizes the importance of personal growth, as the value of the products or services we create is directly tied to the growth in our own character, discipline, and leadership.

Finally, the chapter highlights how Joseph's model can be applied to various business models today—whether in fashion, teaching, or any other industry. The key is to create systems that not only generate immediate profit but also empower others to succeed alongside you, thereby creating a lasting legacy of impact and provision.

Proverbs 13:22 reminds us: *"A good person leaves an inheritance for their children's children."* That's the aim of perpetual revenue: creating a legacy of impact and provision that endures.

Applying Joseph's System for Perpetual Revenue

Joseph's system in Genesis 47 is an incredible example of how to create perpetual revenue, a model that continues generating income long after the initial effort. For a fashion business, this concept can be applied by moving away from a one-time sale model and structuring a system that creates sustainable income.

Creating Perpetual Revenue in Fashion

In fashion, instead of relying solely on one-time sales of clothing or accessories, you can build a revenue-sharing system that continues to generate income over time. For example, consider a model where you design and create high-quality products. Still, instead of simply selling them outright, you invite others to sell your designs or create collaborative collections with you.

- Licensing or Profit Sharing: You could set up a licensing model where other designers or boutiques sell your clothing line under a profit-sharing agreement. For instance, they could keep 80% of the revenue, and you retain 20%. This ensures a steady flow of income as the sales continue without you needing to oversee the process constantly.

- Collaborative Design Partnerships: Another way to apply Joseph's model in fashion is by collaborating with other designers or emerging brands. They can work with you on creating new collections, and you structure the partnership so that both you and your collaborators benefit from the profits. You create a framework where the revenue is shared, much like Joseph did with the people of Egypt.

Empowering Others in Fashion

Joseph's model wasn't about creating dependency—it was about empowering others to succeed. In your fashion business, you can empower designers, stylists, or entrepreneurs by giving them the tools, resources, and opportunity to contribute. Instead of merely creating for the customer, you can also mentor and partner with others in your field, creating an ecosystem where everyone thrives.

- Mentorship Programs: By offering mentorship to new designers or budding fashion entrepreneurs, you provide them with the knowledge and skills to create their own businesses. They, in turn, contribute to your overall success by setting up a shared revenue system, where they give a percentage of their sales back to you in exchange for your support and resources.

- Collaborative Collections: You could team up with up-and-coming designers or artists to create limited edition collections. These collections not only drive interest but also allow the emerging designers to build their reputations while contributing to the continued flow of revenue.

You both benefit from the partnership, and your fashion brand becomes a platform for others to thrive.

Long-Term Revenue Beyond Your Effort

Just like Joseph's system didn't rely on his direct intervention after it was set up, your fashion business can thrive on automated revenue streams. By licensing designs, partnering with others, and sharing profits, your business continues to generate income year after year.

For example:

- Subscription Model: Implement a subscription service where customers receive new items regularly. You can collaborate with other designers to curate new pieces for your customers, while you continue to earn from the ongoing subscriptions.

- Online Courses or Masterclasses: If you teach fashion design or styling, your online courses or masterclasses can be sold repeatedly, creating a continuous stream of revenue without your constant involvement.

Through these approaches, just like Joseph's system, your fashion business can create long-lasting wealth that doesn't depend on a single transaction, but on a system that keeps generating income while empowering others to succeed.

Teaching Business Model: Applying Joseph's System for Perpetual Revenue

Joseph's system of perpetual revenue—creating structures that continue generating income beyond your direct effort—can be directly applied to a teaching business model as well. By shifting from one-time courses or workshops to a shared revenue structure, you can build a sustainable, scalable business that benefits both you and your students.

Creating Perpetual Revenue in Teaching

In teaching, instead of just offering one-off classes, you can create a revenue-sharing model that allows you to continue earning from the value you've already created. Here are a few ways to implement Joseph's system:

- Partnerships with Other Educators: Just as Joseph created partnerships with the people of Egypt, you can collaborate with other educators or experts in the field to co-teach courses, allowing both of you to share in the profits. For example, you might have a co-teaching agreement where you take 60% of the revenue and your co-teacher takes 40%.

- Affiliate Teaching Programs: You can create an affiliate program for other educators to promote and sell your courses. In return, they would earn a percentage of the revenue for every student they bring in. This system not only generates ongoing revenue for you but also enables others to benefit from your expertise, much like Joseph shared the grain with the people of Egypt.

Empowering Students and Fellow Educators

Joseph's model wasn't about taking resources; it was about empowering others to thrive. Similarly, in the teaching business, you can structure your courses and teaching practices to help your students succeed. By empowering others to teach alongside you, you build a network that continuously generates income for all involved.

- Mentorship and Certification Programs: You could offer mentorship programs where you help your students become educators themselves. In exchange for your guidance, they could teach certain sections of your course or lead workshops, and share a percentage of their revenue with you. This allows you to scale your impact while providing your students with opportunities to earn and grow.

- Group Classes and Collaborative Sessions: Instead of teaching alone, consider organizing group sessions where students can interact with one another and contribute to the learning experience. You could share the profits from these sessions with your assistants, helping them build their reputations and careers in the process.

Long-Term Success Beyond Your Effort

Just as Joseph set up a system that generated revenue without constant intervention, your teaching business can continue to thrive long after your direct effort. By implementing a shared revenue model, you ensure that both you and others involved in the learning process continue to benefit over time.

- Recorded Courses and Workshops: Once you've created a course, it can be sold repeatedly. These recorded sessions generate income long after they are recorded, much like how Joseph's grain continued to produce wealth after the harvest.

- Subscription-Based Content: You could create a subscription-based service where students pay for ongoing access to new lessons, workshops, and resources. This creates a recurring revenue stream that grows over time, especially as you bring in more instructors or industry experts to contribute to the platform.

Chapter Six

Honor –To sustain influence and divine favor

Introduction

In Joseph's rise to power, one quality consistently set him apart: honor. He honored his father, Potiphar, the prison leadership, and ultimately, Pharaoh and God. At every level of life, whether in obscurity or in influence, Joseph led with respect, integrity, and humility. That posture unlocked doors no talent alone could open.

Honor, a lifestyle that brings value

Honor is a spiritual principle and relational posture that acknowledges and esteems the God-given value, role, or calling in another person or position. It's important to note that biblical honor is not based on whether a person is perfect or blameless. From a Kingdom perspective, honor is often tied to the position or assignment God has given, not merely to the character of the person occupying it. It involves treating others with dignity, recognizing divine order, and responding to authority, relationships, and opportunity with humility and respect. Honor goes beyond politeness; it is the deliberate act of lifting others, even at personal cost.

In today's culture, however, the value of honor is rapidly eroding. What was once considered a virtue is now often dismissed as a weakness or tradition. The freedom of speech, meant to uphold truth and dignity, is frequently misused as a license to criticize, degrade, and dishonor. Children dishonor their parents; citizens ridicule leaders, and public discourse is marked by sarcasm and contempt rather than respect.

As followers of Kingdom principles, we are called to live differently: to model honor in how we speak, serve, and relate. It is through honor that we preserve legacy, protect unity, and unlock lasting favor.

Biblical Foundation

"Honor all people. Love the brotherhood. Fear God. Honor the king." — 1 Peter 2:17

Joseph's life reveals a key pattern: the more he honored God, the more he honored others, the more God elevated him. When he served Potiphar well, he was promoted. When he honored the prison warden, he gained trust. When he honored Pharaoh, he was elevated to second-in-command.

Joseph's life gives us several specific examples of honor in action:

Honor Toward God (Genesis 39:5; 39:21–22):
Everywhere Joseph went, favor followed him because of his unwavering commitment to honor God. In Potiphar's house, Scripture says, *"The Lord blessed the household of the Egyptian because of Joseph"* (Genesis 39:5). Even after being falsely accused and imprisoned, *"the Lord was with him; He showed him kindness and granted him favor in the eyes of the prison warden"* (Genesis 39:21). Joseph's ability to honor God in every circumstance attracted divine elevation.

This consistent honor toward God fulfilled the principle found in 1 Samuel 2:30: *"Those who honor Me I will honor."* Joseph never credited himself for his success. When interpreting dreams, he repeatedly made it clear that the insight came from God, not his own wisdom. In Genesis 40:8, he told fellow prisoners, *"Do not interpretations belong to God?"* When standing before Pharaoh, he declared, *"I cannot do it, but God will give Pharaoh the answer he desires"* (Genesis 41:16). Later, when reconciling with his brothers, Joseph said, *"It was not you who sent me here, but God"* (Genesis 45:8).

197

Joseph's ability to honor God was also deeply reflected in his willingness to forgive. After everything his brothers had done to him, betraying him, selling him into slavery, and causing their father years of grief, Joseph chose to honor God's command to forgive rather than take vengeance. This act of forgiveness was not only a sign of his emotional maturity but also a spiritual act of honoring God's will and timing. Joseph understood that true honor involves letting go of personal hurt and trusting in God's justice and sovereignty.

Joseph's story teaches us that honoring God is more than just recognizing His presence in the good times; it's about remaining steadfast in obedience and faith through every trial and triumph. His story reminds us that honoring God is not only about praising Him in public but also about following His principles and His word in the hidden moments of life. When we honor God in both good and bad circumstances, we unlock the potential for divine favor and sustained influence.

Honor Toward his father (Genesis 37:13–14):

Even when sent on what seemed like a minor errand, Joseph honored Jacob's instruction and went willingly. His obedience to that small task led to a life-changing journey. Later in life, when Joseph discovered that his father was still alive, he didn't hesitate to honor him. He requested his brothers bring Jacob to Egypt and provided him with the best land in the country—Goshen—ensuring his comfort and well-being.

When it came time for Jacob to die, Joseph didn't rely on his own accomplishments, though he had wealth, fame, authority, and power. Instead, he humbled himself and brought his sons to Jacob to receive a blessing. This act was not about need, but about principle. Joseph understood that honoring one's parents is not conditional on what you lack, but foundational to how you live. He demonstrated that honor is a key to longevity, fruitfulness, and generational blessing. He didn't outgrow honor when he gained position; he deepened it.

Honor Toward his brothers (Genesis 50:14–20):

Joseph was the eleventh of twelve brothers—one of the youngest—and yet bore the deepest wounds caused by them. They betrayed him, sold him into slavery, caused years of grief for their father, and were indirectly responsible for the false accusation that led him to prison. Despite all these injustices, Joseph chose the path of honor, not vengeance. He welcomed his brothers into Egypt, gave them the best land, and ensured their well-being.

What's even more striking is that after their father Jacob died, the brothers feared Joseph would finally take revenge. But Joseph's response was rooted in compassion, spiritual maturity, and an understanding of God's divine purpose. He reassured them, saying, *"You intended to harm me, but God intended it for good to accomplish what is now being done, the saving of many lives"* (Genesis 50:20). This statement not only highlights Joseph's heart of forgiveness but also his unwavering commitment to honor his family, even when he had every reason to retaliate. Joseph's words reflect a deep understanding of God's sovereignty—that what others intended for evil, God could use for good.

This act of forgiveness was a profound expression of honor. Joseph honored God's command to forgive and entrusted God with justice, showing that honor is not just about outward behavior but about heart transformation. By forgiving his brothers, Joseph chose God's higher way—a way that healed broken relationships and opened doors for reconciliation. His integrity outlasted his pain, and his honor elevated not only his family but also God's purpose in his life.

Joseph's story teaches us that honor through forgiveness is not an easy choice—it requires humility, spiritual maturity, and trust in God's justice. In honoring his brothers, Joseph demonstrated that true honor goes beyond what is deserved and reflects the heart of a person who honors God above all.

Honor Toward Pharaoh (Genesis 41:14–16):

Joseph knew that Pharaoh was far from righteous—he had witnessed the harsh policies, executions, and unchecked authority common in ancient Egypt. Yet Joseph understood a profound truth: honor is not about the morality of the individual but about the divine order of the position. He lived with the awareness later echoed by the Apostle Paul in Romans 13:1-2: *"Let everyone be subject to the governing authorities, for there is no authority except that which God has established."* Even when Joseph was elevated to power himself, he maintained a profound respect for Pharaoh and the institution of Egyptian leadership.

Joseph's response to Pharaoh demonstrates this honor clearly. When Pharaoh sent for Joseph to interpret his troubling dreams, Joseph did not seize the opportunity to boast of his own wisdom or abilities. Instead, he immediately pointed to God as the source of his understanding, saying, *"I cannot do it, but God will give Pharaoh the answer he desires"* (Genesis 41:16). Joseph knew that his gift, his position, and even his elevation were gifts from God. He was careful to honor God's plan in how he approached his leadership.

Joseph's honor was also a recognition of the God-ordained authority Pharaoh held. He didn't see Pharaoh's position as an excuse for poor leadership but recognized that God had established him in that role for a purpose. This understanding of the importance of position and authority helped Joseph approach his own leadership with wisdom and respect, even as he exercised great power. In honoring Pharaoh's position, Joseph demonstrated a model of humility that didn't depend on the moral character of the leader but on the divine calling of the office.

Joseph's story teaches us that honoring authority, even imperfect authority, is essential to living in accordance with God's order. Honor for authority does not mean we condone wrongdoing or ignore injustice. Instead, it means we recognize that God has a greater plan, and we submit to His sovereignty over human institutions.

Joseph's ability to honor Pharaoh—without compromising his own values—set him apart and expanded his influence. By honoring Pharaoh's authority and position, Joseph demonstrated a heart that aligned with God's kingdom principles, gaining favor not only with Pharaoh but also with all those around him.

Generosity as Honoring God's Principle.

At the core of generosity is the deep understanding that we own nothing. We came into this world with nothing, and we will leave the same way. Our time, resources, talents, and everything else we possess are gifts from God, entrusted to us for a season. A deeper reflection on life reveals that all we have belongs to God, and He is the valid owner of everything. Generosity, therefore, is not about giving what is "ours," but rather, it is about manifesting God's character and showing that we recognize His lordship over all things. When we give, we acknowledge that everything we have is from Him and that we trust Him to provide for us. Joseph understood this deeply. Even in his rise to power in Egypt, he did not see his wealth and position as his own to keep, but as God's provision to be stewarded. His generosity toward his family, primarily when he provided for them during the famine (Genesis 47:11-12), wasn't just an act of kindness—it was an act of honor toward God. Joseph's giving reflected God's heart of provision, revealing that he trusted God not only to supply his needs but also to use him to care for others. By giving generously, Joseph showed that he cared about God's purposes and sought to manifest His love and grace. In essence, giving is an act of worship, a tangible way to declare that we understand our dependence on God and that we care about reflecting His generous, loving character to the world.

Why Honor Matters for Wealth

- Honor earns trust, and trust builds access.

- Honor protects your reputation, which is one of your greatest currencies.

- Honor attracts partnership, because people want to work with those who uplift and respect them.

In business and ministry alike, honor builds bridges. You can be gifted and still miss out on opportunities if you lack this trait.

This chapter explores how to cultivate a spirit of honor in relationships, leadership, finances, and everyday communication—so that your gift does not outgrow your character, and your influence does not collapse under pride.

Honor isn't weakness. It's the strength to put others first, knowing that promotion comes from God.

Scripture References

Genesis 1:26; 1:28; 13:2; 26:1; 37:13; 39:3; 39:5; 39:21; 40:6; 40:8; 41:9; 41:14; 41:16; 41:33–36; 41:34; 41:39; 41:46; 41:48; 41:49; 41:51; 41:54; 45:7; 45:8; 47:6; 47:11– 12; 47:16; 47:19; 47:24; 50:14; 50:20

Exodus 12:35; 18:13; 25:2; 31:2

Deuteronomy 32:30

1 Samuel 2:30; 16:21; 24:10

1 Kings 17:8; 19:21

2 Kings 4:1

1 Chronicles 25:1; 29:4; 29:14; 29:28

Nehemiah 2:17; 5:14

Esther 8:1

Job 1:1; 1:3

Psalm 148:6

Proverbs 6:6; 12:1; 13:22; 23:7; 30:9

Ecclesiastes 4:9; 10:19; 11:4

Daniel 2:48

Matthew 6:21; 7:24; 14:13; 15:32; 19:24; 20:26; 22:15; 25:14–30

Mark 1:23; 5:1; 9:35; 10:45

Luke 5:1; 5:11; 8:4; 8:43; 16:9; 16:19–31

John 2:1; 5:1; 8:1; 9:1; 11:38; 13:4; 13:14; 14:12; 15:8

Acts 4:32; 4:34; 18:26

Romans 5:7; 12:2; 13:1

1 Corinthians 13:2

2 Corinthians 4:7; 8:9

Galatians 5:13; 5:22

Ephesians 2:10

Philippians 2:7–8; 2:7; 3:7

Colossians 3:23

2 Timothy 2:2

Hebrews 11:25

James 2:26

1 Peter 2:17; 4:10

Collins, J. L. (2016). The simple path to wealth. JL Collins.

Jakes, T. D. (2022). Disruptive thinking. FaithWords.

Maxwell, J. C. (2018). Developing the leader within you 2.0. HarperCollins Leadership.

Toussaint, G. (2020). Hephzibah arise. Shekinah Publications.

Westfall, E. (2023). High road leadership. Tyndale House Publishers.

Contact info

Email   : joseph@twelveseventy.com

Instagram   : @josephtruewealth

               : @elimfinance